BFI TV Classics

BFI TV Classics is a series of books celebrating key individual television programmes and series. Television scholars, critics and novelists provide critical readings underpinned with careful research, alongside a personal response to the programme and a case for its 'classic' status.

Also Published:

Buffy the Vampire Slayer
Anne Billson

Doctor Who
Kim Newman

The Office
Ben Walters

Our Friends in the North
Michael Eaton

For my beloved Catrin (1976–2006).
You will always be 'the girl in all those songs'.

The
Singing
Detective

Glen
Creeber

bfi

First published in 2007 by the
British Film Institute
21 Stephen Street, London W1T 1LN

The British Film Institute's purpose is to champion moving image culture in all its richness and diversity across the UK, for the benefit of as wide an audience as possible, and to create and encourage debate.

Images from *The Singing Detective*, BBC.
Pages 5, 33, 37 – *Stand Up, Nigel Barton*, BBC; page 5 – *Emergency – Ward 9*, BBC; pages 5, 38 – *Casanova*, BBC; pages 5, 79, 80 – *Pennies from Heaven*, BBC; page 11 – *Gorky Park*, Eagle Associates/Orion Picture Corporation; page 25 – *The Third Man*, London Film Productions; page 27 – *Scarlet Street*, Universal Pictures Company/Diana Productions; page 30 – *Carry on Nurse*, © Anglo Amalgamated Film Distributors; page 40 – *Don't Look Now*, D.L.N. Ventures Partnership/ Casey Productions/Eldorado Films srl; page 47 – *The Seven-Per-Cent Solution*, Universal Pictures; page 56 – *Son of Man*, BBC; page 84 – *Track 29*, HandMade Films; page 85 – *Psycho*, © Shamley Productions; page 96 – *Play It Again, Sam*, Paramount Pictures Corporation/Apjac Productions; page 100 – *Detour*, © Producers Releasing Corporation; page 139 – *The Singing Detective* (film), © Icon Distribution LLC.

Whilst considerable effort has been made to correctly identify the copyright holders, this has not been possible in all cases. We apologise for any omissions or mistakes in the credits and we will endeavour to remedy, in future editions, errors brought to our attention by the relevant rights holder.

None of the content of this publication is intended to imply that it is endorsed by the programme's broadcaster or production companies involved.

British Library Cataloguing-in-Publication Data
A catalogue record for this book is available from the British Library

ISBN 978-1-84457-198-7

Set by Fakenham Photosetting Limited, Fakenham, Norfolk
Printed in the UK by Cromwell Press, Trowbridge, Wiltshire

Contents

Introduction

Novelist Stephen King has described *The Singing Detective* (BBC, 1986) as the *Citizen Kane* (Welles, 1941) of the miniseries (King, 2004). Like *Citizen Kane*, its breathtaking and innovative techniques combined with a truly remarkable piece of storytelling make it universal in its themes; dramatically effective and hugely influential. Everything from *The Sopranos* (HBO, 1999–), *Six Feet Under* (HBO, 2001–), *Oz* (HBO, 1997–2003) and Stephen King's own *Kingdom Hospital* (ABC, 2004) owe a debt to it. *The Singing Detective* is not flawless, but its moments of sheer brilliance have come to symbolise the artistic potential of a sometimes downgraded medium. In particular, the serial has become synonymous with 'quality television'; a piece of small-screen drama that is so stylish, challenging and controversial that it equals anything the big screen can offer.

Made by the British Broadcasting Corporation (BBC) in association with the Australian Broadcasting Corporation (ABC), *The Singing Detective* was first shown in Britain over a period of six weeks on BBC1, commencing on Sunday, 17 November 1986. In the week of transmission the *Radio Times* devoted its front page to the series, complete with a lengthy interview with its writer, Dennis Potter, inside. Expectations were unusually high, but the reviews did little to deflate the feeling that this was a special television event. Nicolas Shakespeare declared in *The Times* that 'a man who can create such a dramatisation of his own life, illness and fantasies – and then transform this into an entertaining exploration of the creative process – is quite simply a

Dennis Potter

genius' (1986a: 9). Reviewing the last episode he concluded that it was 'the best thing I have ever seen on television', proving that 'we have only started scratching the surface of what it is possible to do with this medium' (1986b: 9). 'There's television and then there is *The Singing Detective*,' wrote Hugo Williams in the *New Statesman*. 'It's so good your mouth's hanging open' (1986).

    The Singing Detective has also found international popularity in countries such as Germany, Sweden and Australia. In the United States it was first aired on a few PBS stations in 1988 and was later released on the big screen in venues such as New York's Public Theatre. Critics like J. O'Connor of *The New York Times* helped to spread the show's reputation and its popularity grew. Film critic for *The Times* Vincent Canby claimed that Dennis Potter had 'single-handedly restored the reputation of the screenwriter, at least in television. He's made writing for television respectable and, possibly, an art' (1988). Marvin

Kitman of New York's *Newsday* called it 'the most fantastic program I've seen in my eighteen years as a television critic . . . the kind of program that once in a generation comes along and permanently changes the perimeters of what TV drama can do and reclaims it as a creative medium' (cited by Prys, 2004: 183).

One might expect that this sort of praise would have waned since the serial's first transmission. Yet, it still continues to attract considerable critical and public attention. In 2000 it came in at number twenty in the British Film Institute's greatest television programmes of all time and number five in the drama series/serial category.[1] It has also attracted a large cult following that includes some famous fans from Hollywood, such as Martin Scorsese, Woody Allen and Mel Gibson. It was Gibson's production company (Icon Productions) that turned it into a film in 2003 (directed by Keith Gordon and starring Robert Downey Jr and Gibson himself). Although the big screen version only attracted mixed reviews, perhaps it was further testament to the original television serial that seemed to be so perfectly cast, directed and produced that any adaptation would disappoint by the inevitable comparisons.

Although Potter's *Pennies from Heaven* (BBC, 1978) is only one place behind it in the BFI's TV's greatest list, *The Singing Detective* is the piece of work that seems to best sum up Dennis Potter's complex dramatic landscape. According to W. S. Gilbert, it is Potter's '*Hamlet*, his *Ulysses*, his *À la Recherche du Temps Perdu*, his *Seven Pillars of Wisdom*, his *Life and Opinions of Tristram Shandy*, his *White Album*' (1995: 263). In particular, the writer's obsession with the details of his own life (his working-class childhood in the Forest of Dean and his battle with illness); his ambiguous and contradictory relationship with popular culture (pulp fiction, B movies and popular music); his characters' dysfunctional relationship with sex and sexuality (misogynistic, Oedipal, violent); the impact of childhood on adulthood (Rousseauian, Romantic and Freudian) and its densely Christian view of the world (sin, suffering and betrayal) make it a quintessential piece of Potter drama. Its multilayered narrative structure, its use of flashback

3

and montage and its employment of popular music are also evident. In this way, it utilises many of the writer's trademark televisual techniques but with an extra stylistic flourish that has rarely been equalled, even by Potter himself.

The Singing Detective is possibly best understood as the sensational continuation of themes and techniques that Potter had been pursuing and developing since the early 1960s. 'I think any writer', he told Alan Yentob, 'who keeps going over a couple of decades or so is going to be ploughing the same stretch of land whether he knows it or not' (Potter, 1994: 59). In particular, the serial shares similarities with Potter's Stand Up, Nigel Barton (BBC, 1965), a play which employed strikingly familiar childhood scenes (including a classroom betrayal) and even the same actress to play the terrifying schoolmistress.[2] With its use of 1930s popular music and its interests in child abuse, psychiatry and prostitution, Moonlight on the Highway (ITV, 1969) also has strong themes in common with the later serial.[3] The drama also shares similarities with Potter's Emergency – Ward 9 (BBC, 1966) which was similarly set in a hospital; Casanova (BBC, 1971) with its complex structure and its focus on sex, religion and incarceration; and Pennies from Heaven with its characters' tendency to suddenly burst into song. Potter's novel Hide and Seek (1973) also has profound thematic connections with the serial; its male protagonist suffers from the same illness as Philip Marlow and shares many of the same biographical details. Some of these characteristics were also shared by the writer himself and the question of biography (Potter insisted that it was never straightforward autobiography) and its relationship with art is a theme that is explored and examined in both novel and serial.

Despite its narrative and thematic sophistication, the basic plot of The Singing Detective is deceptively simple. Philip Marlow (Michael Gambon), a writer of pulp detective fiction, is a patient in a busy hospital ward suffering from an acute case of psoriatic arthropathy (a debilitating combination of arthritis and psoriasis that Potter also suffered from). As a means of distraction and passing the time he rewrites one of his earlier detective stories (called 'The Singing

Stand Up, Nigel Barton

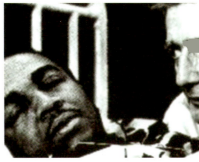

Emergency – Ward 9

Casanova

Pennies from Heaven

Detective') in his head. He also suffers from bizarre and surreal hallucinations (brought about by his illness) and has paranoid delusions about his wife. During memories of his childhood in the Forest of Dean and London we gradually discover the tragic events that informed his early life. However, with the help of psychiatrist Dr Gibbon (Bill Paterson), he gradually begins to realise how his childhood experiences have helped to shape the landscape of his fiction and his fantasies, while also determining his sick and unhealthy view of the world. By its conclusion he is clearly on the road to recovery and is finally able to walk out of hospital, accompanied by his wife (Janet Suzman).

Such a brief description of its basic plot can do little justice to convey the thematic and formal sophistication of the serial as a whole. The way Marlow slowly pieces together the fragments of his life through fantasy, fiction, music, flashback and hallucination is so intricately woven together that it is frequently confusing and deliberately disorientating. However, the incredible achievement of *The Singing Detective* is that all the twists, turns and multilayered narrative worlds do eventually come together. The serial is essentially a psychological whodunnit and its authorial perspective, conflicting generic levels and complex narrative structure are simply designed to allow the audience an insight into the fevered mind of its central protagonist.

As this suggests, *The Singing Detective* is aesthetically and thematically a highly complex piece of work. However, at its centre is a single journey of one man's desperate search for faith and salvation. While the likes of Mary Whitehouse (President of the National Viewers' and Listeners' Association) condemned it for its controversial sex scenes (see Carpenter, 1998: 456), ironically Potter was constructing a deeply spiritual drama that investigated the meaning of religious faith in the contemporary age. It may not be the type of simple religious 'sermon' that Whitehouse and her followers would have embraced, but it is the story of how faith frequently arrives out of the darkest places we inhabit. The framework upon which this all hangs is essentially a Christian one, one man's progress from Eden to Fall and from crucifixion to resurrection. Above all, Marlow must learn to forgive himself for his past sins and alleviate the burden of guilt that is literally crippling him.

Such a reading might suggest that *The Singing Detective* is an intensely worthy, sombre and depressing piece of work. However, Marlow's desperate and isolated suffering does gradually move towards a form of salvation and redemption, one that produces both a cautiously happy ending and a profound sense of hope. Rather than being a pessimistic drama, it is (as perhaps its playful title implies) a work of great 'spiritual optimism' (Cook, 1998: 216). According to Potter (cited by Fuller, 1993: 91):

> *The Singing Detective* was not bleak, in my opinion, in that it attempted to
> show accurately what it is like to be stripped of everything and then to
> attempt, via cheap fiction and a mix of memory – distorted memory,
> invented memory and real memory – to reassemble oneself. It was, in itself,
> a pilgrimage, an act of optimism that began with total nihilistic despair and
> ended with someone walking out into the world.

One of the great triumphs of *The Singing Detective* is also its ability to
set Marlow's intense suffering within a kaleidoscopic array of twists and
turns that helps to keep the story continually fresh and original. Like
any good detective story, the audience is given a number of 'clues' as the
narrative develops, and part of the pleasure of watching the serial is
slowly piecing all of them together until they finally reveal the truth or
'whodunnit'. It might not be a conventional piece of TV detection, but
many of the same generic strategies remain in place in order to keep the
narrative tempo alive and the viewer's curiosity continually engaged.
This is further helped by its ingenious reworking of genres such as film
noir, the Hollywood musical, situation comedy and period drama that
goes to produce a heady array of narrative and stylistic layers.

  The Singing Detective is also very funny, the hospital serving as
a small 'family' around which elements of slapstick, bawdy double
entendres and social satire can take place. Some of the funniest lines
come from Marlow himself – his cynical, misanthropic and scathing
remarks to patients and doctors offer a politically incorrect, scatological
black comedy. As Peter Stead puts it, 'Potter had written a magnificently
witty, crisp, snap-crackle-'n'-pop kind of dialogue that is funny on the
page and quite unforgettable when delivered in Michael Gambon's
plumy and yet silky lounge-lizard drawl' (1993: 110). In one scene
Marlow – as a way of alleviating his skin problem – is being 'greased' by
the beautiful Nurse Mills (Joanne Whalley). Although some of the
references have inevitably become a little dated, the comic absurdity of
the sequence remains intact as he desperately tries to suppress an erection
(18; all future page references refer to Potter, 1986):

7

MARLOW (*voiceover*) Think of something boring – For Christ's sake think of something very very boring – Speech a speech by Ted Heath a sentence a long sentence from Bernard Levin a quiz by Christopher Brooker a – oh think think – ! Really boring! A Welsh male-voice choir – Everything in *Punch* – Oh! Oh!

As confusing as this all sounds, *The Singing Detective* is a deceptively simple story of one man putting the pieces of his life together by examining himself and gradually coming to understand how he can be physically and spiritually healed. It is structurally so complicated and multilayered simply because at the beginning of his story none of this is clear to him and he must search and delve deep into his own confused and repressed unconscious in order to discover who he really is. He is the *real* detective of the story (his fictional detective simply an imaginary alter ego), gradually finding and unearthing 'clues' which will slowly and painstakingly reveal who or what turned him into the sick, angry and faithless wretch that he has become. It is from this point that he must now rebuild his faith, forgive himself (and others) for the 'sins' of the past and learn to take responsibility for his own life. Like John Bunyan's *Pilgrim's Progress* (1687), it is essentially an allegory of Man's religious journey in search of salvation. We follow our pilgrim as he travels an obstacle-filled road, confronted on the way by monsters, spiritual terrors and personal demons, but finally arriving at the gates of the Celestial City.

1 Who Done It?

Very few of the reviews even mentioned me; they called it Dennis Potter's
Singing Detective.

Jon Amiel (cited by Derek Malcolm, 1993)

It is important not to give the impression that *The Singing Detective*
only has one author. While Dennis Potter's remarkable screenplay is an
undeniably significant part of its creation, its interpretation and
transformation into a piece of television drama should never be
underestimated. Making a television programme is always a
collaborative process and to pretend otherwise is to do an injustice to
the profound complexity of the medium that the writer himself so
passionately loved (see Prys, 2006a). Although it is my intention to
primarily concentrate on the textual dynamics of the serial, it is
important that a drama, which is itself partly concerned with the notion
of authorship, should never be reduced to a single authorial source.

Despite the complexity of its production details, the origins of
The Singing Detective inevitably begin with Dennis Potter's script.
Potter began writing for television in the early 1960s, producing
landmark dramas such as *Stand Up, Nigel Barton*, *Vote, Vote, Vote for
Nigel Barton* (BBC, 1965), *Brimstone and Treacle* (BBC, 1976), *Blue
Remembered Hills* (BBC, 1979) and *Pennies from Heaven*. It was after
the success of *Pennies from Heaven* (including a Hollywood remake in
1981 for which Potter's screenplay was nominated for an Oscar) that

pressure was put on the writer to produce a sequel, one that would re-employ the same lip-synch technique that had his characters spontaneously bursting into song. The writer even seems to have pursued this notion for a while, basing an idea for a story around a services' entertainment organisation during World War II.

Although nothing actually came of a sequel to *Pennies from Heaven*, in 1981 a short proposal for a new Potter serial emerged with the title *Under My Skin*. This proposal was, in many ways, very different from *The Singing Detective*, but some of its elements were already recognisable. Like *Pennies from Heaven*, it would include musical numbers and song and dance routines. However, the period of the serial was now changed from World War II to the present day – it was set in a hospital and its protagonist (at this stage called Jack Black) was given Potter's own disease, psoriatic arthropathy.[4] In its conclusion, the proposal argued that it 'will be an uninhibitedly bold attempt by Dennis Potter to use all that he has learned in nearly two decades of writing TV to tell a story that, while remaining inventive fiction, is nevertheless not *too* distant from his own' (cited by Carpenter, 1998: 436).

Originally the idea for the new serial partly came out of Potter's sadness about the demise of the studio TV play in which he had made his name during the 1960s and 1970s. Setting the whole story in a hospital meant that this could be a return to a form of TV drama that he both loved and championed, while also drawing from his own experience. There is no mention of a detective story in this proposal but by the early 1980s Potter had adapted Martin Cruz's novel *Gorky Park* (Apted, 1981) for the big screen, a project that had apparently helped him to rediscover Raymond Chandler's crime fiction. This renewed interest in detective fiction gradually evolved into another idea (entitled *Smoke Rings*), which involved 'a private investigator tracing a missing girl who is believed to have disappeared with a deserter from the American services' (ibid.).

Finally, it seems that both projects began to merge together. It appears that while Potter was keen to pursue more of the serious themes

Gorky Park

of *Under My Skin* (such as hospitalisation and illness), he also wanted to combine that with elements of fantasy and comedy. Potter would later explain that this would hopefully help make the depressing nature of the central story more palatable for an audience (ibid.: 437):

> When I sat down to write *The Singing Detective*, I was uneasy about the project. I continually tried to hold it away, thinking it would be nauseous for the viewer. Then, I thought, write it. Get it out of the system. I couldn't write a horror story, which is what it would have become, so I used all the conventions I like – detective stories, musical, situation comedy.

The script Potter was working upon at that time (Sarah Potter believed her father wrote the first draft in the spring of 1985 [see ibid.: 437]) was originally offered to a number of well-known British directors. These included Stephen Frears, Richard Eyre, Malcolm Mowbray and Pat O'Connor, who were all apparently too busy making movies to even consider directing for television. It was only because of this high rate of refusal that its final director was even considered for the job. Although he would go on to direct big Hollywood movies such as *Sommersby* (1993), *Copycat* (1995) and *Entrapment* (1999), before *The Singing Detective* Jon Amiel had only directed a few television films (such as BBC2's *Silent Twins* [1985]). However, once he had seen Potter's early version of the script (still called *Smoke Rings*) it was a project that he felt obsessively committed to. As he recalls (cited by Hunningher, 1993: 242):

> I remember clearly reading these scripts, and by the time I got half-way through the first script my hands were shaking as I was turning the pages. I knew for absolute certainty because all of my training had been in script development that I was reading a masterpiece. The thought of directing this thing filled me with complete terror and the thought of not being asked to direct it filled me with as much terror.

12

Director Jon Amiel

Amiel's first job after university was as a literary manager at the Hampstead Theatre Club, where he also worked as a director and made his way to the Royal Shakespeare Company. After being fired by Trevor Nunn (because he apparently did not approve of his production of *Twelfth Night*), he decided to move into television and got a job at the BBC, first as a script editor, then progressing on to directing. However, it was perhaps his job as script editor that would prove to be so important for the early development of *The Singing Detective*. After reading the original script, Amiel argued with its writer that significant changes were needed. Potter was not someone whose work had generally been revised in the past and the meetings were, to say the least, confrontational (see Carpenter, 1998: 447–51; Gilbert, 1995: 268–70). However, Potter did finally agree to make the changes that the young director had suggested. Although delighted by this decision, Amiel was dismayed to find out that he intended to rewrite (in longhand) the whole serial only seven weeks before shooting was to commence. 'I remember', Amiel has said, 'this wave of panic and nausea washing over me. What he did was the most amazing feat I've known any writer accomplish ... He literally rewrote every episode from beginning to end. There was not a scene he didn't touch in some way and many he changed dramatically' (cited by Gilbert, 1995: 269–70).

13

The alterations that Potter made to his script at this stage were arguably integral to its subsequent success. They included developing the detective story that originally only appeared in the first episode, strengthening the role of Marlow's wife Nicola and rewriting the final episode so that it became a more successful summation of the previous five. Amiel even persuaded Potter against having the character 'Noddy' revealed as the central manipulator of the drama at its end, a device that he felt was too much like a 'crossword solution' (cited by Carpenter, 1998: 451). According to Potter (cited by Fuller, 1993: 92):

I had lots of chats with the director, Jon Amiel, and obviously he was responding in his way to the material. In between all that, or because of all that, I became aware that I was holding back on something, some sharpness – it needed to be more honest – and Jon's very good at pushing stuff at you or pulling stuff from you, perhaps a bit of both . . . I made Marlow suffer more. I made him more bitter at the beginning, and I made his relationship with his wife stronger, but I also allowed her to attack his evasion in using his illness both as a defence and as a form of attack rather than addressing what was really going on. Small changes in scenes here, there and everywhere would gradually become more dominant, so I would have to rewrite what was around them as well and rethink the emotional trajectory of it.

Changes to the script were also made during production and post-production. Amiel has said about Potter that he 'berated me for some

'Noddy' nearly did it

minor details as we went along, but the truth is that I cut large chunks of text and made considerable changes without warning him and he never commented once' (cited by Gilbert, 1995: 270). This explains why the published script does not always correspond with the TV version, episode five particularly deviating from Potter's original structure. However, the writer did join Amiel for some of the editing process, where they agreed on more changes, particularly increasing the number of associative cross-cuts between the various narrative strands. Potter described this as the 'last and most important rewrite of all' (cited by Carpenter, 1998: 454).[5]

The serial had three producers during its production. The first was John Harris, a BBC series and serial producer assigned by Jonathan Powell at the BBC. Rick McCallum was also employed at Potter's request and began the task of getting the sets built before leaving the production to work on Nicolas Roeg's *Castaway* (1986) (see Cook, 1998: 218). However, Kenith Trodd is most usually referred to as the serial's 'executive' or 'principal' producer and was brought in when it was thought that, having produced Potter's *Pennies from Heaven* (and many other of the writer's productions), he would be able to provide invaluable experience, particularly with regards to the serial's extensive use of music.[6] Trodd and Potter first met during National Service in 1953, continuing their friendship at Oxford University. Knowing him so well meant that he was privy to Potter's personal problems and difficulties, particularly concerning his ill health.[7] It was well known in the industry that they had a volatile relationship but some believed that this mutual aggression may have actually provided a positive framework in which they both could work. According to director Brian Gibson (cited by Carpenter, 1998: 384):

15

Trodd was a great doubter – his strength was to come from a position of scepticism about a lot of things. Dennis seems to have thrived on a certain sort of empowering negativity that he got from Ken. Some writers need to be adored, and told, 'You're a genius'. That was not what Ken gave to Dennis, nor was it presumably what Dennis wanted.

Producer Kenith Trodd

16

On their commentary that accompanies the BBC's 2004 DVD release of *The Singing Detective*, Amiel and Trodd also give credit to a number of other individuals in the production. In particular, Amiel pays tribute to its Head of Photography Ken Westbury, whose camerawork and lighting were hugely important to the way the serial would finally look. Amiel also singles out its editors Bill Wright and Sue Wyatt, who were clearly influential in creating its overall pace and filmic fluidity. The complexity of some of its musical numbers also suggests that the designer Jim Clay and the choreographer Quinny Sacks played significant roles, as well as make-up designer Frances Hannon, particularly for recreating Marlow's dreadful skin condition. Mark Thomas won a BAFTA for his evocative graphics, which begin each one of its opening episodes, crucial in helping to establish its overall tone and sense of style. Thomas also illustrated the cover of Marlow's detective novel, which is seen in the serial and was often used in advertising and promotion of the drama.

Casting was also crucial in creating *The Singing Detective* as we know it today. It is perhaps unfair to single out any individual actors in such an ensemble piece, but Michael Gambon, Patrick Malahide, Janet Suzman, Jim Carter, Alison Steadman, Bill Paterson, Joanne Whalley, Lyndon Davies and Imelda Staunton need to be given enormous credit for giving life to Potter's characters – sometimes a difficult task given the multilayered density of the drama's narrative landscape. One revealing incident involved Patrick Malahide asking Potter's advice on how to play a scene during one of the writer's rare appearances at rehearsals. 'What you've got to understand about this character', the writer told him, 'is that he simply doesn't exist, he's a figment of somebody's imagination.' According to Amiel, he saw the

Photography and lighting by Ken Westbury

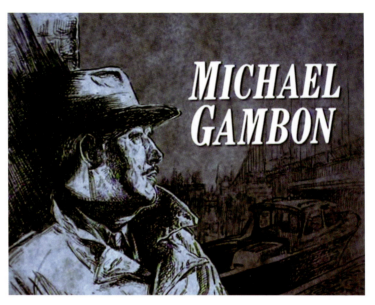

Graphics by Mark Thomas

actor 'completely crumple – all the boundaries he'd carefully constructed just fell to pieces' (cited by Gilbert, 1995: 270).

Although Malahide had the difficult job of playing three separate characters, perhaps the greatest challenge of all came to Michael Gambon in the serial's pivotal performance as Philip Marlow (as both the sick man in the hospital bed and his private eye alter ego). In particular, it was the actor's uncanny ability to capture the combination of anger, cynicism and suffering of Marlow that seemed to make him so perfect for the part (Gambon received a BAFTA in the process).[8] Although admittedly no great fan of Potter's drama, John Caughie admires its central performance (2000: 173):

Gambon's performance gives a depth and a vulnerability to the pain of Marlow which prevents it slipping off the hook with the ironic and protective twist which Potter often gives to his scripts. Imagine *The Singing*

Detective with Denholm Elliott, or Bob Hoskins, or even Nicol Williamson who was originally intended for the part. Carpenter quotes Jon Amiel on Williamson: 'he had the rage, cynicism, irony and eloquence, but he would never make you cry' [1998: 452]. It is precisely the ability to make you cry in Gambon's performance that makes the play of realities matter, registering the experience of young Philip on his disfigured face and *failing* to turn them into melodramatic fiction.

This, all too brief, discussion gives little background to the production as a whole. More general details can be obtained in various sources (see Hunningher, 1993; Cook, 1998; Gilbert, 1995; Carpenter, 1998; BBC DVD, 2004) and will be alluded to throughout this analysis. However, what is important to understand is that, although everything rested on Potter's extraordinary script, the serial was brought to life within an industrial context that few critical accounts will ever fully understand or adequately describe. According to Joost Hunningher, *The Singing Detective* was, above all, 'a creative collaboration' in which even the BBC played its part (1993: 253):

19

Talent does not drop out of the sky, it is fostered and encouraged. Although the series was a relatively low-budget production (about £400,000 per programme), it is not surprising that it was made at the BBC in the mid-eighties when the organisation encouraged confidence in its programme-makers and was comparatively generous in germinating and realising new work.

Although the following analysis will be primarily textual in its approach, I hope that this short account of the origins and production of the serial reminds the reader just how difficult it is to locate a single 'author' for a piece of television drama, particularly one as sophisticated as *The Singing Detective*. This is not to play down the extraordinary contribution of Potter's script, but to prioritise the significance of crucial individuals in bringing that script to life. Jon Amiel certainly needs to be given a great deal of credit, not just for the way the serial finally appeared on screen, but also for his significant contribution to the development and editing of Potter's original screenplay. If any 'author' is to be located at all, then surely it is a joint collaboration between Potter and Amiel. As producer Rick McCallum has put it, 'the two of them made that virtually almost by themselves ... And I mean it's one of the great, great collaborations of all time, between a director and a writer' (cited by Cook, 1998: 218).

2 Structures of the Self

> . . . it is a detective story about how you find out about yourself, how an
> event has lodged inside you and affects how you see things . . . Out of this
> morass of evidence and clues we can start to put up this structure of self.
>
> Dennis Potter (cited by John J. O'Connor, 1988: 30)

There are a number of different generic levels or layers at work in *The
Singing Detective*, all subtly connected and woven together by its
intricate employment of stylistic and narrative techniques. These
narrative levels clash, collide and occasionally completely merge with
each other in such a way that it is sometimes difficult to discern between
them all. The primary reason why this complex narrative structure is
employed is because the whole serial is meant to be regarded as the
projection of one man's thoughts, memories, fantasies and desires. As we
shall see, 'The Singing Detective' novel, the surreal hallucinations, the
childhood memories, the paranoid fantasies (and the place where all
these narrative worlds occasionally meet), is simply meant to be an
articulation of Philip Marlow's troubled mind – constructing an 'interior
landscape' through which all aspects of the story can finally be
understood and explained.

    Before going on to determine how these different narrative
levels and aesthetic techniques reflect the state of Marlow's conscious
and unconscious mind, it is crucial that we first unravel and deconstruct
the serial's complex and frequently confusing narrative structure so that

the very form of the drama is more clearly understood. According to Jon Amiel, the serial can be broken down into four separate narrative levels (BBC, 2005):

> My image for *The Singing Detective* was that it was like a four-storey building. At the basement level were the memories of childhood. On the next floor was our present day story [set in the hospital]. On the next level was the remembered version of *The Singing Detective* script that he wrote. On the top level – the attic if you like – was the place where all of those three different levels somehow – artefacts from them – lay around all jumbled up. And the elevator that shuttled you up between the different floors was the music.

One way to understand how these different narrative 'levels' work is to conceive the device in terms of genre, that is a flaunting of generic categories that seems to deliberately subvert traditional modes of storytelling. Indeed, Potter remembers partly conceiving the serial as a conscious reaction against the inflexible confines of genre that were often applied to his work, particularly during his experience of working in Hollywood on the film version of *Pennies from Heaven*. In a *Radio Times* interview to promote *The Singing Detective* he said,

> [w]hen I was working at MGM . . . they would ask . . . was it a detective story? Was it a musical? Was it a romance? . . . That sort of thinking throws a terrible caprice over the writer and one of the things I wanted to do . . . is to break up the narrative tyranny.
>
> (Cited by Carpenter, 1998: 437)

The very title of the serial certainly appears to implicitly subvert generic categorisation, seemingly connecting the serious and the hard-boiled with the frivolous and the light-hearted.

    The most pronounced use of genre in *The Singing Detective* can be found in the portrayal of Marlow's detective novel. Marlow's surname (without the 'e') is, of course, a reference to Raymond

Four Separate Narrative Worlds (joined together by the songs)	
HALLUCINATORY FANTASIES (including musical and paranoid) Time: present (1980s) Place: in Marlow's head Genre: paranoid fantasy, musical, surreal, hallucination	
'THE SINGING DETECTIVE' NOVEL Time: 1945 Place: London Genre: film noir, hard-boiled detective fiction, crime story	
THE HOSPITAL Time: present (1980s) Place: London Genre: sitcom/medical drama, soap opera, satire	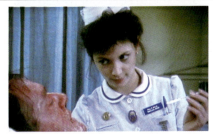
CHILDHOOD MEMORIES Time: 1945 Place: Forest of Dean and London Genre: period drama, family TV drama	

Chandler's hard-boiled detective. 'You'd think my mother would have had more sense than to call me Philip' (21–2), he tells a bemused nurse. His out of print novel (also called 'The Singing Detective') is set in war-torn London, a place seemingly awash with Russian spies, secret agents and double-crossing femme fatales, which are meant to reflect aspects of classic film noir.

The Singing Detective recreates the major characteristics of film noir by employing chiaroscuro lighting, venetian-blinded windows and rooms, urban night scenes with deep shadows, wet asphalt, dark alleyways and flashing neon lights. Ken Westbury's use of lighting is particularly important in these sequences, paying careful attention to shadow and employing low-key (including carbon) lighting. Amiel also seems to have relished the opportunity to indulge in the genre, seemingly paying homage to films like *The Third Man* (Reed, 1949), *Scarlet Street* (Lang, 1945) and selecting background music from over fifty albums with titles like 'Shock Blood Corridor' (Hunningher, 1993: 248–9).

Mark Binney

The Third Man

Marlow's hallucinations also have an implicit connection with this historical period, deriving from the golden age of the Hollywood musical. A musical sequence like 'Dry Bones' clearly plays on aspects of this generic tradition with its Busby Berkeley geometric dance routines and kaleidoscopic choreography, as well as its scantily dressed women and brightly lit sets. As in *Pennies from Heaven*, the musical numbers do not completely transform the set but alterations are clearly discernible. In the 'Dry Bones' sequence from episode one, for example, the hospital ward takes on aspects of Marlow's fictional nightclub so that its signs are now neon-lit and the nurses are dressed as waitresses (ibid.: 243–5). Bars also appear at the windows, perhaps suggesting Marlow's sense of personal imprisonment. Potter's original script simply set this scene in a dark void with actors wearing skeleton costumes; therefore much of the credit for the style of these musical sequences must go to Amiel, the designer Jim Clay, the choreographer Quinny Sacks and the costume designer Hazel Pethig (see Hunningher, 1993).

Lili

The influence of more contemporary musicals such as *All That Jazz* (Fosse, 1979) is also apparent in some of these sequences. Perhaps taking his cue from Federico Fellini's *8½* (1963), Bob Fosse's film moves from realistic dance numbers to extravagant flights of cinematic fancy as its dying protagonist meditates on his life, women and death. It even has musical numbers set in a hospital, involving sequences that are similar in style to *The Singing Detective*, particularly in their pronounced use of hands and shoulders in the dance routines and their undercurrent of eroticism. Although often used in hallucinations, the songs also appear more 'realistically' in Marlow's childhood and as period numbers in 'The Singing Detective' story, but even here (as in 'The Umbrella Man' sequence) they are sometimes performed in a style that would not be out of place in an old MGM musical.

Although perhaps not as obvious, there is a discernible use of

Scarlet Street

28

'Dry Bones'

genre in the hospital scenes. Mr Hall (David Ryall) and Reginald's (Gerard Horan) constant bickering provides a 'Greek Chorus' to Marlow's story but also a comic double act that has echoes of classic British sitcoms like *Steptoe and Son* (BBC, 1964–73), *Doctor in the House* (ITV, 1969–70) and *Only When I Laugh* (ITV, 1979–82). However, there is also a much darker strain to some of the humour on offer here, the serial having much in common with political satires such as *The National Health* (Gold, 1973) and *Britannia Hospital* (Anderson, 1982), where the medical institution is seen as a metaphor for a nation.[9] But much of the humour would not be out of place in bawdy British comedy films like *Carry On Nurse* (Thomas, 1959) and *Carry on Matron* (Thomas, 1972), Potter's script not afraid to exploit the hidden embarrassments of hospital life and the seemingly endless possibility for sexual innuendo. As this brief exchange suggests (8–9):

All That Jazz

> REGINALD: Mr Hall thinks something ought to be done about it –
> MR HALL: (*Sidelong Hiss*) Shut your mouth, Reginald.
> REGINALD: – By the time *we* get it, the tea's either cold or stewed to buggery –
> STAFF WHITE NURSE: Language!
> MR HALL: (*Quickly*) But very welcome you are miss, in *this* bed. Whichever way you turn.
> *And then a tiny moment of horrified silence from him, as he takes the full measure of his hapless double entendre.*[10]

Of course, these institutional scenes are also reminiscent of hospital soap opera, complete with their fair share of flirtation, melodrama and life and death suspense. One of the more pompous doctors is even named Dr Finlay (Simon Chandler), an explicit reference to *Dr Finlay's Casebook* (BBC, 1962–7), which gave early British television viewers an idealised version of the medical profession (see Jacobs, 2001: 24). Some of the hospital scenes actually derive from an earlier Potter play called

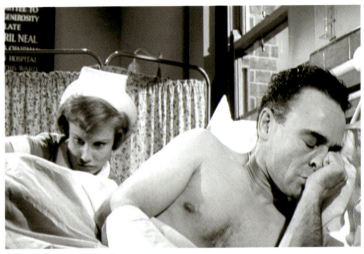

A bed bath in *Carry On Nurse*

Emergency – Ward 9, which (as its title suggests) was partly a satire on
the hugely popular medical drama *Emergency Ward – 10* (ITV,
1957–67). Filmed entirely in a studio, *Emergency – Ward 9* (which now
exists only in script form) included strong elements of sitcom and what
John R. Cook describes as 'tough-minded humour' (Cook, 1998:
211–12). Indeed, Potter's love affair with studio drama meant that he
initially urged Amiel to film the hospital scenes in a television studio and
on video. However, this was a request that was denied for various
reasons, not least the inability to make a seamless join between video and
16mm film (see Fuller, 1993: 93–5). The scenes were finally shot on film
in an abandoned hospital in Tottenham, North London.

Other genres include a version of 'period drama' in the
childhood scenes, reflecting and utilising some of the pleasures evoked
by watching historically based British television drama like *Upstairs,
Downstairs* (ITV, 1971–5), *Shine On Harvey Moon* (ITV, 1982–95)
and particularly children-centred historical films like *The Railway
Children* (Jeffries, 1970). Although Potter had a well-known dislike for
the term 'nostalgia' (see Fuller, 1993: 22–3), there is an undeniable

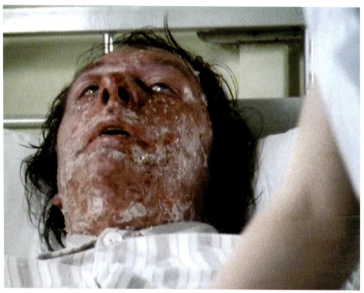

A greasing in *The Singing Detective*

enjoyment evoked in *The Singing Detective*'s use of steam trains, historical dress and its employment of period music – indeed, the songs from the serial produced a number of best-selling albums.[11] There is clearly a great deal of green, grey and brown employed in this narrative world, suggestive of images found in old sepia photographs and evoking an essentially warm *mise en scène*. There is a darker side to these childhood sequences that one would not expect to find in such genres (particularly of a sexual nature), but much of it would not be out of place in an early-evening small screen family drama. As we shall see, there are strong religious undertones to these scenes that also make it particularly suited to Sunday, the day in the UK when it was first broadcast.

The way these different genres connect, collide and merge into each other is perhaps also suggested in its casting. The same actor often plays different characters in the various narrative stories. The most obvious example is Michael Gambon, who plays both the bedridden

Period drama

Marlow and his hard-boiled alter ego, 'The Singing Detective' (our sleuth is also a singer in a dance band). This also applies to Patrick Malahide, who we first see as Mark Binney (a spy in Marlow's detective novel) but who also plays Raymond Binney (Mrs Marlow's illicit lover in the childhood flashbacks) and Mark Finney (Nicola Marlow's imaginary lover). Other examples include Alison Steadman's role as Mrs Marlow and Lili; Joanne Whalley's role as Nurse Mills and the nightclub singer Carlotta; Trevor Cooper's part as a barman and a cloth-capped local in a working-men's club and Kate McKenzie's part as Sonia and a prostitute visited by the real Marlow.

This cross-referencing in terms of casting is not only contained within the boundaries of the text itself. Those familiar with earlier Potter drama will notice Janet Henfrey, who not only plays the schoolmistress in *The Singing Detective* but played a remarkably similar role in Potter's earlier single play, *Stand Up, Nigel Barton*. Although

Janet Henfrey: in
*Stand Up, Nigel
Barton*; as the
schoolmistress; as the
scarecrow

Amiel states on the DVD commentary (episode three) that this casting was done mainly because of the particular qualities of the actress, its associations are nonetheless apparent. To make matters more intertextual, Henfrey also plays the frightening 'scarecrow' in the young Philip's vivid imagination.

While not all the actors play different roles, they are rarely entirely contained by their narrative space. Often characters from one story will suddenly appear in another narrative 'level'. As the serial develops so this narrative convergence becomes increasingly more pronounced, finally climaxing with the Two Mysterious Men (Ron Cook and George Rossi) lost in Philip's childhood forest and the fictional hard-boiled detective coming face to face with his creator in hospital. This breakdown between 'real' and 'fantasy' adds a dense narrative texture to the serial as a whole and produces a 'heightened reality' where all things seem connected and all worlds are joined by an inherently intertextual subtext. For example, one of the recurring images of *The Singing Detective* is of a woman's dead body being pulled from the River Thames. We see this image several times and each time it is slightly altered as the body mutates into various different identities, alternating between Mrs Marlow/Lili, Nicola Marlow and Sonia.

This means that there is little that can be trusted on face value in *The Singing Detective*. The serial produces an unstable sense of place, time and identity that is essentially fluid and dream-like. Consequently, there is an almost 'avant-garde' feel to it that is unusual for television, which tends to rely heavily on realism for its success in genres such as soap opera or documentary (see Tulloch, 1990: 117). In particular, it seems to reflect some of the work of the French New Wave (*nouvelle vague*), especially the work of directors like Jean-Luc Godard and Alain Resnais who took a somewhat experimental approach to film-making. Resnais's *Hiroshima, mon amour* (1959) and *L'Année dernière à Marienbad* (*Last Year at Marienbad*) (1961), for example, both displayed a non-traditional structure which completely dispensed with chronological time – a technique that tended to produce an elliptical sense of past, present and future. Interestingly, Resnais later became

Sonia

Nicola Marlow

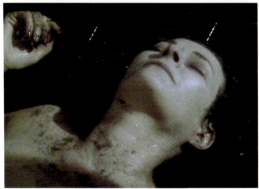

Mrs Marlow

such a fan of Potter's drama that he made *On connaît la chanson* (*The Same Old Song*) (1997) after the writer's death as a tribute to the man and his work.

The Singing Detective's blurring of fact, fiction and fantasy is particularly heightened by its recurring and pronounced use of montage. Montage is an approach to editing first employed by the Soviet film-makers of the 1920s and later developed by the likes of D. W. Griffith. Dissolves, fades, superimpositions and wipes are often used to link the images in a montage sequence. They are sometimes employed to compress a passage of time, summarise a topic or suggest what a character may be thinking. Such devices are frequently used by Amiel, Bill Wright and Sue Wyatt, often as a way of seamlessly moving from one narrative world into another and constructing a landscape where there has been a blurring of normal categories such as reality and fantasy.[12] Aural montage is also an important element in creating this apparently seamless flow of events. The noise of a train, the regular bleep of a heart monitor or the bars of a popular song helping to merge or interlink one scene with another, bringing images and sounds together in such a way that we sometimes barely notice the gentle shift between one narrative level and another (see Prys, 2006b).

Montage and dissolves are most strikingly used in *The Singing Detective* as a device to visually illustrate Marlow's thoughts (whether they are memories, fantasies or hallucinations). This use of montage as subjective perspective was a recurring trademark in much of Potter's drama, a technique he used as early as 1965 in *Stand Up, Nigel Barton*. For example, there is a moment in the opening few minutes of the play when Nigel's (Keith Barron) face is superimposed over a freeze-frame of his father (Jack Woolgar). This appears to signal to the audience that we are entering into Nigel's memory, a suggestion that is heightened by the fact that his childhood self is played by the same actor who plays him as an adult. Unlike a traditional flashback, this seems to explicitly indicate that we are entering into Nigel's consciousness, the montage sequence suggesting to an audience that we are moving to a subjective and highly personal point of view (see Creeber, 1998a: 47–57).

It was probably Potter's six-part serial *Casanova* that used montage most elaborately. It is possible to view *Casanova* as an earlier 'draft' of *The Singing Detective*, the constant shifting in flashback, flash-forward, fantasy and hallucination makes it structurally very similar. It also shares many of its central themes – sexuality, religion and incarceration (see ibid.: 158–66). Towards the end of his imprisonment its central protagonist even suffers from a dreadful skin condition. Like Marlow, Casanova constantly revisits memories from his earlier life (particularly his endless sexual conquests), often revealed in a complex array of visual montage. As TV critic Nancy Banks-Smith explained at the time, she enjoyed 'the shapely swing of the thing, the night–day, waking–dreaming swing between his imprisoned despair and the liquid idyll of a love remembered in flashback' (cited by Carpenter, 1998: 269).

This characteristic use of montage has particular similarities with the work of British film director Nicolas Roeg. Such were their

37

Stand Up, Nigel Barton

Casanova

similarities that they even collaborated together to make *Track 29* in 1987. In particular, Roeg and Potter's work seems to share an interest in portraying the fluidity of time; intent on revealing how the past, present and future are intimately linked and connected. Sections of Roeg's *Don't Look Now* (1973) are particularly reminiscent of *The Singing Detective*, most notably its array of recurring images that are almost 'subliminally' edited into the film's *mise en scène*. One of the most memorable sequences in Roeg's film is of a dead woman's body being pulled out of a river. As in Potter's serial, its central protagonist (Donald Sutherland) has lost a member of his close family (his daughter) through drowning and therefore the scene has a particular resonance for him. This is clearly implied by a quick edit to the earlier tragic event as he watches the woman being pulled from the river. In this way, the association between past, present and future is suggested through the grammar of the film itself.

However, there are important differences between the use of editing and montage in *Don't Look Now* and the type that we find in *The Singing Detective*. Whereas Roeg's film seems to suggest a 'metaphysical' or 'supernatural' connection between these disparate images, Potter's script appears more concerned with making *psychological* associations. As in earlier Potter productions, the suggestion is that we are meant to view much of the drama through the eyes of its central protagonist. At times Marlow's face is superimposed over scenes from his childhood or his detective novel as we dissolve from one narrative level to another, signalling to an audience that they are entering his mind. Similarly, in the hallucination sequences we are frequently given shots of Marlow responding to what he sees while other patients (not involved in the hallucination) carry on as normal, oblivious to what he is apparently witnessing. In this way, montage,

The Singing Detective

Don't Look Now

dissolves and point-of-view shots help produce an 'interior monologue' through which we are able to be privy to Marlow's secret thoughts and fantasies.

The fact that all the complex layers of the narrative may well be connected by our central protagonist is signalled early on in episode one. As part of 'The Singing Detective' novel, we follow Mark Binney into a wartime nightclub, where he is met by a barman. 'G'evening, sir,' says the barman, 'what is your poison? What'll be, sir? *Ouch-h-!*' (4). This sudden grimace (the barman inexplicably doubles up in pain) seems to have no logical source in the detective story, but in a quick edit to the present day we see that the true source of the pain is actually from the real Marlow himself, suffering from an uncomfortable wheelchair ride through a long hospital corridor. 'Concentrate', he says to himself, 'Concentrate' (ibid.), a clear sign to the audience that he is the author of the story we have been watching and that its narrative is somehow offering him a form of escape from his present painful circumstances.

'Interior monologue'

A further hint of the serial's subjective perspective is given just a few minutes later when the extent of Marlow's skin condition brings disgusted reactions from the other patients. Although it is clearly impossible for him to have overheard their abusive comments, he seems strangely able to recount their every word to himself. According to the published script 'he imitates *exactly* what he mostly cannot possibly have heard. That is, he lip-synchronizes precisely to the real voices' (6). Potter's use of the 'lip-synch' term here (usually applied to his characters' habit of miming to pre-recorded songs) suggests the way the drama as a whole is meant to be viewed. We are explicitly directed to see the series through Marlow's 'authorial' perspective.

Perhaps the most striking example of this narrative subjectivity comes in episode four, when Nicola and Mark Finney are seen planning to steal Marlow's screenplay. 'I know this sounds crazy,' Finney tells Nicola, 'I feel almost as though he has made this all up' (147). Later they even provide the appropriate punctuation and stage directions to their speech and movements as if they were reading from a script. 'I have this awful – ', Finney explains, 'I have this awful dash he stops himself comma and all but shudders full stop' (149). As we later discover, Marlow has indeed made up the whole paranoid fantasy and his own invented characters are beginning to suspect it. What this reveals is that he is the pivotal focaliser through which every scene and narrative level must be read. The techniques (compelling and complex as they are) are simply a means of delivering what Potter has referred to as his tendency towards 'first-person narrative' (Potter, 1994: 12).

This may explain how and why popular music plays such a pivotal part in 'shuttling' the narrative between different generic levels. Not only do all the songs come from the period in which Marlow's detective novel is set but also his childhood. This means that they can move from memory to detective novel and to hallucination with ease. In this way the music is used in an explicitly 'Proustian' manner, the opening chords of a song immediately taking Marlow back in time or reminding him of a particular part of his story.[13] This suggests just how intimately connected each narrative level actually is. Just as the music moves from one level to another, so do the faces, the places and the characters, thus revealing a complex narrative universe in which everything is connected by a single authorial perspective.

This is one way of making sense of all the various narrative levels and generic forms that are at work in the serial as a whole. All the different stories are connected because they all arrive out of the same central imagination, one that is painstakingly going over past events and rewriting earlier stories in a desperate process of self-examination. The drama offers an essentially subjective trajectory – everything is meant to be understood from the point of view of Marlow and every single image, dialogue, sound and song comments in some way on him and his present condition. Marlow is the narrative centre of the serial and everything is seen (sometimes explicitly 'written') through his eyes. The childhood flashbacks, the detective narrative, the paranoid fantasy involving his wife, even many of the apparently 'naturalistic' hospital scenes are clearly meant to be deciphered through the texture of his conscious and unconscious mind.

There were initiatives early on in its production to shoot the detective elements of the story in black and white and the rest in colour, but it was generally agreed that this may have helped viewers to discern each narrative world far too clearly. It was also partly for these reasons that the hospital sequences were finally shot on film in a real location, the scenes shot on video in a studio would have offered too much of a contrast to the filmed sequences. The blurring of generic boundaries is, as we shall see, an essential element of the story, it is not just the structure on which the narrative hangs but is also an essential part of its thematic content. As its use of montage suggests, Marlow is lost in a landscape of his own making; his present circumstances are so unbearable that he retreats into a 'twilight world' where reality, memory, fantasy and hallucination have become increasingly blurred. 'Sometimes', he tells Nurse Mills, '. . . these hallucinations – they're even better than the real thing' (21). This is the personal universe that he (and the audience) must unravel together, to find out the truth of Marlow's present unease among the plethora of real and imaginary worlds that besiege him.

This helps to explain why Potter makes the narrative landscape of *The Singing Detective* so multilayered. Although a chronological trajectory would have been far easier to follow, it would not have allowed us access into the confusion that is Marlow's inner realm. In particular, this narrative structure would seem to be linked to the nature of human consciousness, especially the notion of repression. Our hero begins his journey in a profound state of denial; he does not want to face up to the reality of his present situation or the painful memories of his past. Indeed, the rewriting of the detective story is initially part of this repressive process in that it is designed to take his mind off his current unhappy state. However, escapist pulp fiction and popular music will ironically lead its author back to his own life and his deeply buried psychological problems. Rather than diverting him away from his troubles, popular culture forces him (albeit indirectly) to actually confront himself.

This is what Sigmund Freud calls 'condensation' and 'displacement'; the notion that dreams (and therefore, implicitly, all stories) can be read as metaphors for repressed desires. This is something that the psychiatrist Dr Gibbon seems acutely aware of – he even brings a copy of Marlow's detective story to their first therapy session. With the help of psychoanalysis, Marlow is suddenly forced to face up to memories and desires that he had hitherto repressed, his own story being a source of great personal insight. The period songs are also emotionally potent as they will take him back to where he least wants to go, to his own painful childhood memories. Nevertheless, the therapy, the novel and the songs do slowly force him to confront what he has tried to repress for so long. As Potter told Graham Fuller (1993: 87):

> . . . the cheap fiction, the illness and the cheap songs – well, not so cheap – were together conspiring to force him to recognise what he was: stark, stripped down, with nothing but a ferocious rhetoric, plus self-pity. Because the pain was so great he was trying to think of 'The Singing Detective' novelette that he had written, and trying to rewrite it simply as an exercise in not going mad. That in turn led him to start assembling his life, and the songs were part of that assemblage.

Seen in this context, the crime genre allows Potter to make explicit connections between crime fiction and psychoanalysis. 'When I grow up, I be going to be – a detective,' Philip declares as a nine-year-old boy high in a tree. 'I'll find out. I'll find out who did it!' (77). In this way, the detective story becomes an allegory for the therapeutic process and it is this psychological 'whodunnit' which is the true subject of the story. To be 'cured' Marlow has to literally find out who (or what) are the reasons for his present sickness. Appropriately enough, the detective story follows a similar trajectory to the psychoanalytic procedure; they both begin with an enigma or mystery (crime/neurosis) and through a slow process of investigation (detective work/therapy) they try to uncover its underlying cause (who or what was to blame).

Such connections between psychoanalysis and detective fiction may seem overly exaggerated. However, as both became popular in the late nineteenth and early twentieth century it is understandable that they could be seen as deriving out of a similar set of social conditions, particularly the rise in the use of scientific methods to understand all aspects of the natural world. This may help explain the origins of Conan Doyle's Sherlock Holmes; a fictional and extreme portrayal of scientific reason applied to human behaviour. As John Fraim explains, it is therefore not surprising that Freud was a great fan of Conan's creation (Fraim, 2002):

> Just like his literary hero Sherlock Holmes, Freud came to see the world composed of clues and hidden meanings concealing a great mystery. In a large sense, Freud's *Psychopathology of Everyday Life* (1901) was a detective manual, finding evidence or 'clues' to the mystery of personality in everything. Freud in effect modelled much of his system on this emerging detective fiction, becoming a sleuth like Sherlock Holmes. A literary genre was appropriated to the emerging psychology of the unconscious. Perhaps more the case, Freud's system mirrored an emerging popular literary genre of the time.

This connection between psychoanalysis and the detective story is not unusual in contemporary film and literature. A novel by Nicholas Meyer

45

called *The Seven-Per-Cent Solution* (1974) even dramatised a
fictionalised meeting between Sherlock Holmes and Sigmund Freud.
Made into a film of the same name in 1976, it was directed by Herbert
Ross, who went on to direct Potter's film version of *Pennies from
Heaven*. It even starred Nicol Williamson as Sherlock Holmes, the
original choice to play Philip Marlow.[14] Like *The Singing Detective*, *The
Seven-Per-Cent Solution* clearly exploits the connection between
psychoanalysis and the detective story. The similarities between the
book/film and Potter's screenplay are profound. Narrated by Mr
Watson, this discussion between Freud and Holmes (while the great
detective is under hypnosis) suggests strong similarities between Holmes'
and Marlow's particular childhood traumas (Meyer, 1974: 215):

> 'Why did you become a detective?'
> 'To punish the wicked and see justice done.'
> 'Have you ever known injustice done?'
> There was a pause.
> 'Have you?' Freud repeated . . .
> 'Yes' . . .
> 'Have you known wickedness personally?'
> 'Yes.'
> 'What was that wickedness?'
> Again the subject hesitated and again he was encouraged to answer.
> 'What was that wickedness?'
> 'My mother deceived my father.'
> 'She had a lover?'
> 'Yes.'
> 'What was the injustice?'
> 'My father killed her.'

Holmes' childhood trauma in *The Seven-Per-Cent Solution* is strikingly
similar to Marlow's; they both have mothers who are unfaithful to their
husbands and who die as a direct consequence. Although Mrs Marlow
commits suicide and is not murdered (she throws herself from

The Seven-Per-Cent Solution

Hammersmith Bridge into the Thames), the psychological and emotional context is not dissimilar. In particular, both scenarios have distinctly 'Oedipal' connotations. In the 'Oedipus Complex' Freud famously argues that the original Greek myth (which concerns Oedipus unknowingly marrying his mother and killing his father) taps into and articulates unconscious fears and desires that all male children have around the age of five years old. The complex (which is a normal and essential part of a boy's psycho-sexual development) has him fixating on his mother and competing for her attention with his father, who he unconsciously wishes dead (see Freud, 1930).[15]

Interestingly, *Oedipus Rex* is often referred to as the first ever detective story, 'the story of a master detective in search of the master criminal' (Meter, 1976: 12). In this sense, the detective story becomes a site through which these unconscious childhood desires are played out, the detective punishing the wicked and pursuing justice as a way of absolving himself of his past 'crimes'. In other words, the repressed and guilty desires of early childhood are re-enacted in dramatic form so that they can be re-expressed and controlled. As Charles Rycroft puts it, the detective 'is living a fantasy of being in omnipotent control of the internalized parents' (cited by ibid.: 19). 'I'll get you,' Marlow's detective hisses as he holds the dying Lili (played by the same actress who plays Mrs Marlow) in his arms. 'Whoever you are. Whatever you are. Wherever you are' (125).

It is this connection between psychoanalysis and detective fiction that *The Singing Detective* so explicitly explores and exploits. Bedridden and virtually unable to move, Marlow has no option but to uncover 'clues' to his psychological neurosis. These 'clues' come in many forms – they may appear in the memories and popular songs of his childhood or in his detective novel or in his paranoid fantasies about his wife – but they all lead back to one source, himself. 'I know the clues are supposed to point in the direction of the murderer,' Gibbon tells him. 'But what if they also reveal the victim a little more clearly' (52). There is certainly a complex puzzle to be solved by Marlow and his long and troubled investigation is one that needs to go over and over the same old ground; that is, until the mystery of the 'crime' has been solved. As Therese Lichtenstein explains, this is why *The Singing Detective* has to be told in such a strikingly non-linear manner (1990: 171):

> The way Philip combines memories, fictions, fantasies, and actual perceptions is closer to our own thought patterns than is the conventional linear narrative. The viewer is placed in the role of detective, the quintessential voyeur, putting together shards of evidence, clues that slowly start making sense. It is as though Freud had met Columbo in a psychological thriller, their purpose to reveal the monad of Philip's identity.

Issues surrounding detection and psychoanalysis and the precise details of Marlow's own psychological neurosis will be discussed in more detail in the following sections. However, what should be apparent now is how the generic form of the story and its filmic grammar is implicitly linked to its content and to its particular portrayal of personal consciousness. The serial is not just about *one* man's long journey from denial to recovery, but is implicitly the narrative of all our lives and the way in which we slowly piece them together (sometimes from only fragments of memory, fantasy and reality). 'The worst thing about a detective story', Marlow explains, 'is the plot . . . You have to work it all out in your head. And that's what I've been trying to do. Like a rat in a maze' (139). Marlow is the detective in all of us, a man simply wondering how to make sense of the greatest mystery of all; his own life.

3 Sins of the Flesh

All the days wherein the plague *shall*
be in him he shall be defiled; he is unclean: he shall dwell alone; without the
camp *shall* his habitation *be*.

Leviticus (emphasis in the original, 13: 46), KJV

The first episode of *The Singing Detective* is called 'Skin'. In the opening few minutes we see the doorway of a nightclub called Skinskapes.[16] A doorman appears, he wipes a stain off the back of his right hand and we hear the opening bars of 'I've Got You under my Skin'. These references to skin immediately bring us to the very heart of the story and to the core of its central protagonist's illness. Marlow's outer and inner landscape has literally become a 'skinscape', a world preoccupied and obsessed with aspects of the flesh. As this suggests, skin lies at the very centre of this extraordinary narrative. To really understand the psychological terrain of this serial we need first to remind ourselves of the important role that skin plays in our physical, cultural and emotional lives. This is the key motif that will unlock the psychological and religious context of the work around which so many of its central themes and dramatic techniques revolve.

Although the phrase 'skin deep' tends to suggest that the skin is entirely on the surface of the body, it is well known that the organ can sometimes reflect feelings below the outer layer or epidermis. If we are

Skinskapes

embarrassed our faces may blush or a sudden rash may suggest hidden anxieties. Indeed, it is believed that many skin conditions may often be a reflection of trouble (or 'dis-ease') elsewhere in the body or the mind. This maybe one of the reasons that they have frequently been treated with such terror and trepidation; not only is there the fear of infection through touch but also the skin may be seen as reflecting personal or psychological problems. Historically, skin conditions were often seen as some form of divine retribution for sins committed in this life or a past one. Of course, this link between sin and disease is not unique to skin conditions; in the *Book of Common Prayer* sin is described as 'no health in us'.[17] However, there is something peculiarly personal about the skin that seems to make its affliction more socially shameful than other conditions.

Perhaps the erogenous nature of the skin means that it is particularly prone to associations of wickedness or 'the sins of the flesh'. When Adam and Eve realise they have sinned they are suddenly ashamed of their nakedness. First, they hide their genitals with fig leaves, but then God makes them 'coats of skin' to cover the rest of their naked bodies. It is also the serpent that tempts Eve, a creature known for its damp, scaly skin, which it can shed. These are connections between skin and sin that go back many centuries and are perhaps even suggested in their linguistic similarity – s(k)in.

These sinful associations may partly explain why skin conditions have been treated with such shame in the past. Leprosy, for example, has been considered one of the more despicable of diseases and sufferers of it were shunned for many centuries. Sometimes kept in separate places such as leper colonies and sanatoriums, if lepers were free to move around then they were ordered to ring a bell or rattle a clapper to warn people of their presence. As leprosy was contagious and untreatable in biblical times it was seen as a terrible plague; its cure was often linked with great miracles and contact with a leper defiled whoever touched them. So, while the treatment of other diseases is called 'healing' in the Bible, the treatment of leprosy is frequently called *cleansing*. Thus, leprosy has become synonymous with the loathsome and 'the unclean'.

The social consequences of having a skin problem are therefore sometimes as great – if not greater – than the condition itself. Sufferers of skin conditions may feel acutely self-conscious about their appearance and subsequently suffer from depression, low self-esteem and a fear of public rejection. If only unconsciously, sufferers may even feel as if their condition is some form of retribution for past misdemeanours. In short, the skin is a complex and unique piece of human biology: it reveals our outer and inner selves; it is part of our cultural, social and sexual identity; and it can frequently determine and influence our relationship with ourselves and others.

Philip Marlow suffers from an extreme case of psoriatic arthropathy, a combination of two separate complaints that affect both the skin and the joints. While the 'arthropathy' refers to arthritis (the painful inflammation of the joints), the 'psoriatic' refers to the skin condition psoriasis (grey or silvery flaky patches on the skin which are red and inflamed underneath). Depending on the severity and where it occurs, individuals may experience significant physical discomfort and some disability. Many people have psoriasis in a mild form but in extreme cases the sufferer is entirely covered in lesions. Being scaly and flaky means that the condition is often described as 'snake-like'.

It was this disease that Dennis Potter suffered from for all of his adult life. The writer's arthritis was so acute that his hands and fingers were permanently closed tight. While purely a medical condition, these permanent 'fists' became a potent symbol for many critics of Potter's aggressive and frequently abrasive personality. The unofficial biography by W. Stephen Gilbert is entitled *Fight & Kick & Bite* (1995) and the playwright's official website goes under the title of 'Clenched Fists' (see Dave Evans [2006]). It was clearly a very painful and debilitating illness that led to bouts of anger, depression and social isolation. Frances Hannon (the make-up designer on the serial) remembers how Michael Gambon's simulated psoriasis was toned down just before shooting. This was because there were fears that the full extent of Potter's condition may have actually made viewers switch off (see Hunningher, 1993: 247). This is how Potter described the arrival of the disease when he first experienced it in his early twenties (cited by Fuller, 1993: 12–13):

> It was like one of the plagues of Egypt! With 100 per cent psoriasis you lose control of your body temperature. You semi-hallucinate. You're in danger of septicaemia, and therefore you're in danger of dying. People say they've got psoriasis, and they mean they've got some really uncomfortable itches, which won't hurt and don't make the skin flake off. With the extreme psoriatic arthropathy that I have you can't find a point of normal skin. Your pores, your whole face, your eyelids, everything is caked and cracked and bleeding, to such a degree that without drugs you could not possibly survive. It was physically like a visitation . . .

Potter's references to 'the plagues of Egypt' and 'visitations' are revealing because of their biblical connotations. Although psoriasis is not contagious and is actually thought to be hereditary, in Roman and biblical times it was often mistaken for leprosy. In Leviticus a man is covered in a 'white' skin condition that covers his entire body. This was probably psoriasis because leprosy is not white and rarely covers the whole of the body (except in its later stages). However, these biblical associations between skin and sin are significant and appear to make Marlow's illness particularly rich in Christian symbolism. All of these issues are clearly not lost on Dr Gibbon who quickly identifies his patient's deeply rooted feelings of guilt and shame (55–6):

> Most chronic dermatological patients are on tranquillizers or antidepressants, you know. Almost as a matter of routine. The skin, after all, is extremely *personal*, is it not? The temptation is to believe that the ills and the poisons of the mind or the personality have somehow or other erupted straight out on to the skin. 'Unclean! Unclean!' you shout, ringing the bell, warning us to keep off, to keep clear. The leper in the Bible, yes? But that is nonsense, you know. *Do* you know? Well – one part of you does, I'm sure.

54

As this suggests, the illness that Potter bequeaths on his troubled protagonist is not just one he knows intimately, it is filled symbolically with a heady cocktail of religious faith, sin, sickness and salvation. It is also an illness that seems to have a direct correlation between Marlow's outer and inner self. His 'dis-ease' may manifest itself on the skin but the problems that have caused this condition appear to run much deeper – their origins firmly located in the 'sins' of his past and particularly his traumatic childhood.

We learn about Marlow's childhood through intermittent flashbacks that slowly unravel over the six episodes, gradually increasing as Marlow's therapy and self-reflection intensifies. Many of these scenes were shot in the Forest of Dean, a small rural community on the border between England and Wales where Dennis Potter was himself brought up.[18] The Forest of Dean is still quite a remote place, but during Potter's childhood it was particularly insular. 'I grew up in a wholly enclosed coalmining community,' he told Graham Fuller, 'which is geographically isolated as well; in sophisticated metropolitan terms you could even call it "backward" ' (cited by Fuller, 1993: 5). It is certainly a recurring presence in Potter's work and is rich with metaphorical as well as geographical significance. As Fuller puts it (ibid.: 1):

> This ancient royal forest of oaks and ferns, grazing land and orchards, small coalmining communities with Free Church chapels and working-men's clubs, lies between the rivers Severn and Wye, just east of the Welsh border. It is the Arden of Potter's childhood and suggestive of a psychic landscape in his work as Monument Valley is in John Ford's Westerns.

The Forest of Dean was a strongly religious community at the time of Potter's birth. Only forty miles from Shakespeare country, its language was reminiscent of biblical English. 'Thee' and 'thou' were still then the most common ways of saying 'you' (ibid.: 5).[19] 'While not strictly Puritans,' writes John R. Cook, 'most of the Foresters were non-conformist Christian fundamentalists – chapel-goers who dutifully filed into stone buildings with names like Zion and Salem in order to be ignited inside, by the hell-fire sermonising of the local Preachers' (Cook, 1998: 8). As a child Potter even remembered giving certain landmarks biblical names: 'the big ponds near the pit where Dad worked was Galilee. The Valley of the Shadow of Death was a lane descending between overhanging hedges . . .' (ibid.: 4–5). He argued that the Forest of Dean was even detectable in *Son of Man* (BBC, 1969), his most overtly religious drama, which reinterpreted the story of Christ (cited in ibid.: 38):

> For me, *Son of Man* obviously nods back to the Forest of Dean, the chapel, the strength of those biblical images in my mind, and my assumption that

> Jesus – the carpenter's son, the Galilean wanderer – was a rebel. It had
> something to do with childhood memories, the most vivid one in terms of
> literature being from the New Testament and Salem Chapel, that kind of
> thing. The Forest of Dean is a place where such a wondrous creature would
> have roamed.

Not surprisingly, a great deal of Potter's work often connects the Forest
of Dean with biblical imagery and Christian associations. In particular,
it is often portrayed as an innocent paradise or 'Garden of Eden' (even
their names have a passing similarity). In *Pennies from Heaven* Arthur
(Bob Hoskins) finally meets his 'angel' Eileen (Cheryl Campbell) there,
the first letters of their Christian names suggesting the Bible's first
couple, Adam and Eve. Similarly, in *Blue Remembered Hills* the forest
becomes a natural and organic playground for his group of unruly but
essentially innocent children, at least before its tragic conclusion. The
Forest also plays a central role in his last two posthumous serials
Karaoke (BBC/C4, 1996) and *Cold Lazarus* (C4/BBC, 1996), where it is
affectionately renamed the 'Forest of Nead', seemingly reflecting the
writer's constant desire for it (see Creeber, 1998b).

This appears to be the kind of world that the nine-year-old
Philip Marlow (Lyndon Davies) spies upon from the high branches of

Son of Man

his beloved oak tree. The way Amiel has the camera slowly pan over the tops of the trees (dense, green foliage completely fills the screen before resting on Philip) heightens the intense naturalness of the location. In a grey sweater and light brown shorts the boy is, at first, barely noticeable among the branches, perhaps as natural as the trees themselves. He sees a ladybird on the branch and he lets it crawl over his hands, taking great care not to harm it. Although the fact that he is alone in the tree does suggest that he is already a little isolated and lonely, it is still a rare glimpse into the boy's brief harmony with nature. It is from this natural vantage point that we see Philip reciting the Lord's Prayer, suggesting perhaps that he is also in communion with God. In Potter's earlier novel *Hide and Seek* (1973), its protagonist Daniel Miller (who also suffers from psoriatic arthropathy) remembers having a religious epiphany high in the boughs of a tree as a child in the same forest. From his heavenly vantage point he suddenly sees that 'God was not a word in a book or a gigantic figure in the sky. He saw that God was things, was in and of things, every sort of thing, breathing through them, breathing out of them' (Potter, 1973: 110).

Although we detect in the young Philip's slightly aggressive manner that innocence is soon to be lost, for the time being he can only dream about adulthood in very childish terms. 'When I grow up,' he tells us in direct address to camera, '... I be going to have a whole tin of evaporated milk on a *whole* tin of peaches I be!' (77).[20] In this childlike state he even refuses to accept that he will one day die. 'I be going to be the first man to live forever and ever,' he tells the camera. 'In my opinion, you don't have to die. Not unless you want to. And I byunt never going to want to' (ibid.). Things are not entirely stable in his world, yet he is still willing to put his trust in God. 'When I grow up, *everything* ... ool be ool right ... Won't it God? Hey? Thou's like me a bit – doosn't, God? Eh?' (ibid.).

As this ominous note suggests, the boy's fragile paradise is about to be disturbed. He spies two people weaving their way through the undergrowth beneath him. As a place rarely frequented by adults this is immediately suspicious. The sight of this couple certainly appears

57

to agitate him and he now places the ball of his thumb over the ladybird and kills it. Turning to the camera he tells us, 'I cont abide things that creep and crawl and . . . I cont abide dirt' (113). The 'creeping and crawling' Philip speaks of is mirrored by this couple's careful and illicit progress through the forest, while the reference to 'dirt' seems to suggest that this type of behaviour appears 'dirty' or 'unclean' to the boy. The Forest dialect of the couple and their talk of 'devils', 'angels' and 'apples' certainly suggest a religious subtext, Raymond even pricking himself on a thorn that attaches itself to the woman's dress. In particular, the scene has echoes of the Christian Fall, the moment when, persuaded by the serpent (a word from Old French meaning 'to creep'), Eve succumbs to temptation (112):

> MRS MARLOW: You've been here before, haven't you! This is not the first time –
> RAYMOND: (*Leer*) I byunt say nothing.
> MRS MARLOW: Oh, you dirty devil, Ray. You're not good, Raymond.
> RAYMOND: Ah. But that's what you d'like, yunnit? You don't want no angel doost?
> MRS MARLOW: Don't think so much of yourself. There's always another apple in the barrel.
> *He laughs, pulling her away.*
> RAYMOND: Come th'on, then. Let's see the pips!

When the nine-year-old boy carefully climbs down from his tree to get a better look, he witnesses his mother (Alison Steadman) having sex with Raymond Binney (Patrick Malahide), the father of a boy from Philip's school. By prematurely witnessing the sexual act his innocence is dramatically shattered, his movement from the tree tops to the forest floor reflecting his 'fall from grace'. The tree that was once a symbol of his Eden has now become the tree of knowledge. It is upon this single scene that the whole serial essentially revolves. It arrives in the middle of the third episode and at the very centre of the drama, suggesting its pivotal place in the narrative as a whole. It is a crucial

Paradise lost

moment around which the whole story and the story of Marlow's life revolve.

Of course, this was one of the most controversial scenes in *The Singing Detective* as a whole. The *Today* newspaper heard about its content before it was broadcast (Trodd thinks Potter may have actually tipped them off in order to boost ratings) and demanded that Michael Grade (the then Director of Programmes at the BBC) be forced to 'order cuts'. After an 'emergency meeting' was organised, Grade accepted that the scene was vital to the plot and no changes were made (see Carpenter, 1998: 455–5).[21] It was a brave decision for the BBC but the publicity certainly did the drama no harm, after starting out with around 8 million for the first three episodes it acquired around 10 million viewers for the second half. However, the controversy was still running a year after the serial was first aired when MP Gerald Howarth prepared a Private Member's Bill aimed at extending the Obscenity Laws to cover Broadcasting. Playwright Alan Plater was consulted as part of a Writers' Guild delegation and found that much of his time was spent defending *The Singing Detective* against people who had only seen 'edited highlights' of the series (provided by Mary Whitehouse).[22] Plater argued that this scene was integral to the drama as a whole and would have made little sense without it. As he put it (1992: 78):

> Sex . . . recurs throughout the history of drama and its importance, almost invariably, is in its effect on other people: tragically in Othello, where the sex takes place in the mind of the protagonists: farcically and off-stage in Feydeau or Ben Travers; but traumatically and necessarily on-screen in Dennis Potter's The Singing Detective, where the boy's glimpse of his mother's extra-marital sexual encounter is a crucial element in a complex, multi-level narrative.

60

Indeed, the fall-out from this simple act of betrayal is everywhere in *The Singing Detective*; Philip is never the same again and all his further actions seem an unconscious response to it. In his innocence the sexual act appears 'akin to violence or physical attack' (113), making it a terrifying and traumatic experience for the boy. Like Adam and Eve, he is suddenly struck by the 'sinfulness' of the body. Scared and confused, he will later secretly go back to school and defecate on the desk of the schoolteacher. As strange and disturbing as this behaviour may seem, it is perhaps Philip's only way of venting feelings deep within him that he does not properly understand. According to Freud, if witnessed by a child, sex is not only mistaken for violence but also with other bodily functions (Freud, 1977: 335):

> If children at this early age witness sexual intercourse between adults . . . they inevitably regard the sexual act as a sort of ill-treatment or act of subjugation: they view it, that is, in a sadistic sense. Psycho-analysis also

> shows us that an impression of this kind in early childhood contributes a
> great deal towards a predisposition to a subsequent sadistic displacement
> with the problem of what sexual intercourse . . . consists in: and they
> usually seek a solution of the mystery in some common activity concerned
> with the function of micturition or defaecation.

Of course, Philip's schoolmistress (named only as 'Old Woman' in the
published script) is disgusted by what she discovers on her desk. She
particularly appears to equate it with something bestial. 'Cows do it in
the fields', she furiously tells her class, 'and know no better. Dogs do it
in the road and know no better. Pigs do it in their sties and know no
better' (138). This difference between the human and the animal
kingdom reflects a general theme in Genesis (after The Fall Adam and
Eve lose their 'Divine Consciousness' and become more like 'the beasts
of the field'). Of course, there are sexual connotations to this descent
from Divine to animal. In *Paradise Lost* (1667) Adam compares sexual
love to 'carnal pleasure' and animal copulation, 'think the same
voutsaf't/To Cattle and each beast' (Milton, 2001: 192). Prematurely
faced with the sexual act, Philip knows only too well that some people
behave just like animals. However, the schoolmistress clearly believes
that the Christian message teaches us to rise above such basic instincts.
'But *we* are not animals,' she implores, '. . . God has given us all the
sense of good and of bad . . . *God* has allowed us to tell the difference
between the clean and the dirty' (ibid.)

Unfortunately, Philip is now clearly confusing the difference
between the 'clean' and the 'dirty'; the organic paradise of his youth is
suddenly transformed into a fallen and filthy world. When he kills the
ladybird (frequently a symbol of innocent nature) he alarmingly
mistakes nature for 'dirt', a confusion that appears to eventually
consume him. This morbid state of mind could be likened to the 'Slough
of Despond' in the *Pilgrim's Progress* (1687), the murky swamp on the
way to the Wicket Gate into which the pilgrim falls and sinks under the
weight of his burden, that is his own sin and guilt. At times Marlow
appears to believe he is in a similar dilemma, his whole world

descending into an unclean and decaying state. 'I have occasionally seen patients who are just as bad and sometimes worse than you are,' explains the Registrar (Thomas Wheatley), 'but they don't behave as if they've fallen into a sewer' (39).

It is when the young Philip visits London with his adulterous mother that he shows her his 'first psoriatic lesion' (185). The filth he equates with the natural world has now finally been transferred to his own flesh, the psoriasis making his body seem 'dirty' and 'unclean'. 'I'll put some Zam-Buck on that,' she says, before telling him to 'pull' his 'sleeve down' (ibid.), suggesting an early and ominous hint of shame. Expelled from 'Eden' and cast adrift in a dangerously urban landscape, in a few moments Philip will run, terrified, into the deep stairwells and corridors of the London underground as if it were the underworld. For it is here that he finally tells his mother what he had witnessed in the forest. 'Doing that stuff. With thik Mr Binney. With Raymond Binney. Mark's Dad . . . Him on top of tha! Rolling about on top of tha! . . . Shagging' (186). Stricken with shame and guilt for what she has done she later commits suicide by throwing herself from Hammersmith Bridge.[23]

As we shall see, Mrs Marlow's suicide firmly connects 'sex' with 'death', but it also explicitly implicates the nine-year-old boy with these tragic circumstances. The first 'psoriatic lesion' becomes a Mark of Cain, Philip perhaps feeling he has 'killed' his mother as Cain murdered his brother. It is symbolically a mark of shame, a human stain that will always remind him and others of his 'sins'. When Philip returns from London without his mother he is met at the station by his grief-stricken father (Jim Carter). In the forest Mr Marlow naturally tells his boy that he loves him. 'Shh!' his son replies. 'Somebody might hear us' (222). While mimicking the illicit lovemaking of his mother and Raymond, the disturbing comment also vividly reveals the shame he now associates with feelings of love. Inexplicably, Philip runs away from his confused father and hides in his forest tree. It is reminiscent of the moment when Adam hides from his 'Father'. 'I heard thy voice in the garden', Adam says, 'and I was afraid, because I was naked; and I

Underworld

hid myself.' Puzzled by this, God asks, 'Who told thee that thou wast naked?' (Genesis, 3: 10–11).

This action also echoes the earlier moment when Philip ran away from his mother after their argument in the London underground. He is physically and emotionally turning away from his parents, hence their repeated calls of 'Philip! Philip!' that continually punctuate the narrative. As he illicitly watched his mother in the forest behaving 'like an animal', he now secretly sees his father let out 'one long and strange and almost animal-like cry of absolute grief and despair' (233).[24] The world has now completely transformed for the boy, and from earthly paradise Philip is gradually descending into hell.

Like Cain, these terrible events transform Marlow into a fugitive, and he withdraws into a world where those who love him can no longer hurt him. 'Don't trust anybody again!' he says to himself. 'Don't give your love. Hide in yourself. Or else they'll die. They'll die. And they'll hurt you. Hide! Hide!' (232). The skin becomes the means

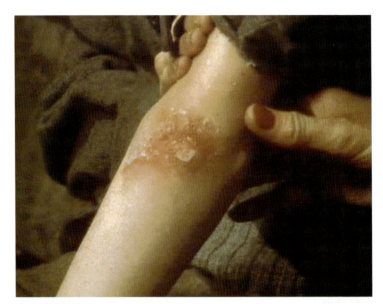

Mark of Cain

Hell

by which Marlow retreats into himself; a way to keep people at arm's length and not allow them to get too close. No longer wanting to be part of society he constructs a means of solitary confinement, sinking into an illness that is shunned by the rest of humanity. '[Y]ou use your illness as a weapon against other people', his wife angrily tells him, 'and as an excuse for not being properly human.' (218).

After the events in the forest and the death of his mother a void opens up between Philip and his father, a divide made all the more difficult through his gradual movement into education and away from his working-class roots. At one point we see Mr Marlow singing in a working-men's club (ironically, he is accompanied by his wife on piano and her illicit lover, Raymond). The adult Marlow also imagines himself to be there but realises he cannot applaud his father's singing like everyone else in the room because the arthritis in his hands has left them permanently clenched. 'You byunt interested in clapping thee father, now be ya?' says one of the locals to him. 'Thou's never did give the poor bugger credit when him was alive! Got too big for thee boots, disn't' (Potter, 1986: 78).

Marlow's precise psycho-sexual condition will be explored in more detail in the following section. However, what is most important to understand here is that an enormous amount of guilt is now working on the young boy's fragile and tortured mind. Unconsciously believing he is to blame for his mother's death, he is riddled with self-loathing and appears to take the sins of the world onto himself. '*My fault,*' he tells himself. '*Me. It's me. Me. It's all my doing. Me. It's me. My fault. Mine. Our Father which art in Heaven Hallow'd be thy name ...*' (70) (emphasis in the original). In this sense, Marlow's psoriasis can also be seen as a form of self-punishment for earlier 'sins'. According to psychiatrist Otto Fenichel, 'outbreaks of psoriasis in particular may represent sadistic impulses turned against one's ego' (1966: 225). 'What are you doing here?' Nicola asks him in hospital. 'Oh, punishing myself,' Marlow replies (194).

The overwhelming guilt that the young Philip now feels will gradually spill out into all aspects of his life, not least his experiences at school. Determined to find the culprit who has soiled her desk, the cane-wielding schoolmistress interrogates her class by literally putting the fear of God into them. Asking the children to close their eyes tightly and pray, she conjures up the image of a terrifying and omniscient Deity who knows and sees *everything*. It is a fire and brimstone rant worthy of any fundamentalist preacher. As arthritis is an inflammatory auto-immune disorder that causes the immune system to attack the bones, her 'sermon' takes on an ominously prophetic meaning for Philip. 'Dear Lord', she rants, '*You* can see. *You* know ... You are looking down now upon one boy, one particular boy, one boy in this room ... You are entering the bones. You are peering in the space between the bones. Dear God. Almighty God. Terrible in Wrath' (144).

Detecting Philip's unease during her speech the schoolmistress makes him stand out at the front of the class. As an intelligent boy (to add to his growing sense of shame his classmates tease him with taunts of 'Clever Dick' [76]), she can not believe it was him who actually did it, but suspects he knows something about the 'crime'. As he stands there, stricken with fear, she continues a science lesson about the structure of the leaf, hoping that the boy's resistance will finally break. Of course, the topic of the lesson brings us straight back to the source of Philip's biblical Fall. Interestingly, she also compares the leaf to the human body and explains that it has 'veins', 'ribs' and '*bones*' (emphasis in the original: 164). Such a description implicitly connects Philip's fear and guilt with aspects of his own body. Indeed, she heightens the shame he already feels as her terrifying tactics force him to blame another classmate. Later, Marlow discovers to his horror that the boy he blames (it is the son his mother's lover, Mark Binney [William Speakman]) will finally end up in psychiatric care, only adding to an already profound sense of guilt. It is a Judas-like act of betrayal, a treacherous deed that will live with him for the rest of his life. While Philip's mother betrays his father with a kiss, so he points the finger towards the innocent in a similar act of treachery.

Seen in this context, 'God's Wrath' seemingly enters Marlow's

Betrayed with a kiss

body and his appropriately 'snake-like' skin becomes a result of biblical damnation, his sins literally written on the body. As a middle-aged man crippled with psoriatic arthropathy in hospital, Marlow looks surprisingly Christ-like in bed, he is even dressed in a 'tiny loin cloth', which the script insists is 'normal practice when seeing a dermatology consultant' (24). Perhaps one way of looking at it is that his childhood oak tree has now turned into a cross on which he is metaphorically 'nailed' and 'crucified'. However, as in the Bible, crucifixion is followed by a resurrection and Marlow is finally redeemed and able to walk out of the hospital with his wife by his side.

   This journey through hell (from Eden to Fall and from crucifixion to resurrection) is the very essence of *The Singing Detective* and a fundamental part of its underlining religious structure. In particular, there is a deep biblical impulse at the heart of the narrative

Eden

Fall

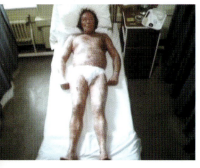

Crucifixion

Resurrection

that concerns a paradise lost and a desperate struggle to leave the bodily sins of the world and return to innocence. No matter how difficult it is, it is ironically Marlow's skin that finally makes him look at and examine what is going on below its surface. Only when he starts to do this can he begin his long and painful road to recovery and redemption.

The feelings of shame, self-loathing and isolation that many sufferers of skin conditions feel is reflected in the title of a recent book called *Don't Fence Me In: From Curse to Cure, Leprosy in Modern Times* (2005). According to its author, Tony Gould, during the 1940s the last leper colony (or 'leprosarium') in the United States latched onto Bing Crosby's version of 'Don't Fence Me In' and made it their own (see

Gould, 2005: 2), seeing it as a comment on the way that society unfairly rejects and excludes people with the illness. It would later be the same song that is played in *The Singing Detective* to accompany the young Philip in the forest as he sits high in his tree reciting the Lord's Prayer. At that moment Philip is not 'fenced in' and can roam the countryside at will, perfectly in tune with Nature and God. However, the things that he sees in the forest will forever taint his view of the world and isolate him from his own body. The skin, the most normal and natural symbol of human life, becomes a profound source of shame for Marlow and a symptom of his terrible unease. In his troubled mind 'skin' and 'sin' become intimately related, resulting in a severe neurosis that will transform both his psychological and biological landscape.

4 Women, Sex, Death

> Woman is the archetype of the oppressed consciousness: the second sex.
> Her biological characteristics have been exploited so that she has become
> the receptacle for the alienation all men must feel; she *contains* man's
> otherness, and in doing so is denied her own humanity.
>
> Juliet Mitchell, *Psychoanalysis and Feminism* (emphasis in the original,
> 1974: 123)

In the previous section Marlow's complex psychological history was
investigated. However, the actual form of his neurosis and the way in
which it manifests itself in his imagination needs to be more thoroughly
explored if the thematic intensity and coherence of *The Singing
Detective* is to be better understood. In order to appreciate these issues
more clearly we need first to uncover the details of Marlow's
psychological anxieties; a complex mental landscape that constructs and
determines his distorted view of women and sex. In particular,
Marlow's sexual psychology appears to display explicitly Freudian
undertones. This is not to say that audiences are expected to passively
accept such a psychoanalytical reading, but that Marlow's emotional
condition seems to have archetypal origins that Freudian psychoanalysis
may help us understand in more detail.

Such is the narrative and thematic complexity of *The Singing
Detective* that psychoanalytical readings can sometimes be reductive
and simplistic. However, the explicitly Freudian structure of the serial

(the understanding of the self through therapy and intense self-reflection) means that it would be foolish to completely disregard such interpretations. Indeed, as Paul Delany suggests, Marlow's miraculous recovery at its conclusion almost turns the serial into a 'commercial for psychoanalysis . . .' (1988: 518). What is certainly clear is that his early sexual development was somehow altered and influenced by what he witnessed at the age of nine in the forest. His relationship with his mother is transformed and will eventually influence his relationship with women as a whole. Sexually and emotionally immature, he retreats into a world of fantasy and fiction that reflects his distorted view of the world.

By accidentally witnessing the primal scene as a young boy, Philip's world is made to feel dirty, a biblical sense of being 'unclean' that is even transferred onto his own body (in the form of psoriasis and arthritis). However, just as importantly, it also introduces the notion of death into his organic paradise, for it is his confession to his mother about what he saw in the forest that prompts her suicide. In this way the sexual act is implicitly linked to death in his mind (a death that he now unconsciously blames himself for). It is a profound 'fall from grace', the young boy's premature witnessing of sexual intercourse dramatically shattering his prepubescent innocence and subsequently bringing about a tragic awareness of his own mortality. Despite what he once said high in the bows of his beloved tree, he now knows he will not live for ever. This too has biblical connotations, as death is the direst consequence of Adam and Eve's disobedience. According to Genesis, Adam and Eve would have attained absolute perfection and retained immortality had they succeeded in withstanding temptation. 'Dust thou art', says God to the sinful couple, 'and unto dust shalt thou return' (Genesis, 3: 19). When God kills an animal to clothe the sinful couple this further introduces death into the Garden, a seemingly innocent victim of their guilt and shame.

The connection between sex and death is heightened by the way the primal scene is remembered by the adult Marlow, temporarily confusing it with the death of George (Charles Simon), an elderly patient

71

Sex and death

in the hospital bed next to him. The scene of the doctors trying to resuscitate this dying man is carefully intercut between the couple's lovemaking, the thrust of their bodies perfectly mirrored by the medical staff's desperate attempt to keep the man alive. As Raymond climaxes noisily on top of Mrs Marlow so George is pronounced dead. 'It's over' (114) says a voice from the emergency team, implicitly connecting sex and death in dramatic style. It is one of the few scenes in the serial where sex is portrayed as mutually pleasurable. 'Oh, stay in me' (114), Mrs Marlow tells Raymond as he starts to pull out of her.[25] However, that feeling of intimacy and arousal soon disappears when he boastfully tells her, '[o]ne more done, then' (ibid.). 'You're heavy Raymond,' she suddenly complains, as she realises she's just another one of his conquests, '. . . [g]et off! Get off me – Raymond!' (115). Now filled with shame and regret she suddenly bursts into tears. As elsewhere in Potter's work, the pleasure of sex is not only fleeting but is usually followed by a brutal *petite mort* ('little death').[26]

Although referenced as a 'slug or an insect' (ibid.) in Potter's published script, the choice of a *lady*bird as the insect that Philip kills while perched in his tree is particularly appropriate as the scene will forever influence his relationship with the opposite sex. In particular, it would appear that Marlow now blames *women* for his fallen state. This eventually leads him to develop a deep misogyny, one that has been informed by an Old Testament view of women, with his mother taking on the role of the temptress Eve. Indeed, feminists have criticised Genesis because it casts the female as such a treacherous figure, while also implicitly blaming all women for the problems of the world. Such a reading also argues that the female figure is always seen as secondary or inferior to Adam (his 'Other'). This was reflected in the title of the feminist magazine *Spare Rib* in the 1970s, an allusion to the fact that God made Eve from one of Adam's ribs. Feminists argued that this suggested she was simply a by-product (or an appendix) of the male species, rather than being an individual in her own right (see Zoonen, 1994: 22).

It is this kind of biblical misogyny that Marlow appears to be

73

Snake in the grass

consumed by. As his father was betrayed by his mother so he starts to
believe that no woman can ever be trusted – hence the problems in his
marriage and his paranoid delusions about his wife and her (imaginary)
lover, Finney. This perhaps explains why Patrick Malahide decided to
make his character so 'snake-like' in appearance (see BBC, 2005), as
Finney is the creature who ultimately tempts Nicola to betray her
husband (at least in Marlow's sick imagination). You can also detect
this sort of biblical theme in Marlow's detective story. When Binney first
walks into Skinskapes he is not aware that a female companion will
soon join him at his table. However, the barman informs him that he
will get 'the pick' of the 'apples on the bough . . .' (4). As this implicit
biblical reference suggests, all the women he meets there are (like Eve)
untrustworthy. As it turns out, they are actually a combination of
prostitutes and Russian spies, so the barman's implicit description may
be uncannily correct.

The misogyny in Marlow's detective story will be discussed in the following section, but what is important to understand here is its psychological source. At the root of Marlow's distrust of women is, inevitably, his mother's betrayal in the forest. Most children would be traumatised by witnessing the primal scene, but the fact that his mother is not with his father makes it a further act of treachery. '*Wos him a-doing?*' Philip thinks to himself, '*[w]os him doing to our Mam? Mum! Mum! Shall I go and fetch our Dad?*' (emphasis in the original: 115). This link between sex and betrayal is later vividly suggested when Gibbon reads a passage to the writer from his detective story where sexual intercourse is described in disturbing and traumatic terms. 'Mouth sucking wet and slack at mouth,' he reads, 'tongue chafing against tongue, limb thrusting upon limb, skin rubbing at skin . . . Faces contort and stretch into a helpless leer, organs spurt out smelly stains and sticky betrayals.'[27] Marlow's only response to the reading is an angry 'Oink. Oink' (120). Instead of being associated with love and tenderness, sex has now become associated with an act of guilt, one that is filled with feelings of betrayal and animalistic desires. Consequently, the skin is no longer a source of pleasure but a site of discomfort and disgust. As in Genesis, the flesh suddenly becomes a profound source of shame.

75

These biblical associations are later explicitly revealed in a word-association game that Marlow 'plays' with Gibbon. The cutting between the doctor and his patient as their words are exchanged clearly heightens the dramatic tension of the scene. In particular, the increasing tightness of the composition and the grim realisation of discovery that is signalled in Gibbon's slow turn to Marlow at its climax is revealing. It leaves us in little doubt of the significance of their dialogue, the shock on Marlow's face clearly discernible at its close. 'I don't think I'll come here any more,' he quietly announces. In terms of the words exchanged, notice particularly how Marlow's references to 'women', 'fuck', 'dirt' and 'death' are preceded by associations of the crucifixion ('nail', 'cross', 'passion'). Man's sins against God are somehow transferred into 'sins of the flesh', with distrustful women ('pretence') ultimately at their root (177):

MARLOW: Humbug.
GIBBON: Cant.
MARLOW: Can!
GIBBON: Tin.
MARLOW: Tack.
GIBBON: Nail.
MARLOW: Cross.
GIBBON: Passion.
MARLOW: Pretence.
GIBBON: Woman.
MARLOW: Fuck.
GIBBON: Fuck.
MARLOW: Dirt.
GIBBON: Dirt.
MARLOW: Death.

Similar associations between women, sex and death can be found throughout *The Singing Detective* as a whole, referred to explicitly (as in the word association game) but also in more implicit forms. As is suggested in this brief exchange between the young Philip and a group of soldiers he meets on the train that is returning him from London alone (207):

FIRST SOLDIER: Where is she? Eh? Where's your Mum, your lovely Mum?
PHILIP: In the ground.
FIRST SOLDIER: Oh, yes?
PHILIP: Yes.
FIRST SOLDIER: Covered in dirt?
SECOND SOLDIER: That was always on the cards.
FIRST SOLDIER: Covered in the old dirt. Her legs and all. Eh?
The soldiers laugh, nastily, as in a bad dream.
PHILIP: Yes. Covered over.
They stop laughing and stare accusingly at him.
FIRST SOLDIER: You done it. Didn't you? It's all your doing, Sonny Jim.

Marlow's view of women and sex has been forever tainted by the forest incident, the sexual act now associated in his mind with feelings of guilt and shame.

In this sequence his mother is not only spoken of in implicitly sexual terms ('Her legs and all . . .'), but is also explicitly connected with dirt and death. Sex has been transformed in his eyes from a natural to a filthy act, and one which will always result in tragic circumstances. In his unconscious mind women are to blame for this, so they must (as his mother was) be punished. This is a common theme in much of Potter's work as a whole. It is usually the women characters who take the blame for tempting men into sex, almost always resulting in violence against them and occasionally resulting in their death (see, for example, *A Beast with Two Backs* [BBC, 1968]). In Marlow's paranoid fantasy about Nicola she is cheating on him as Mrs Marlow cheated on his father (the nude painting of her hanging in Binney's and Finney's apartments perhaps a blatant reminder of her predatory ways). She therefore has to be punished, Finney finally betraying her with violent consequences.

It is this distrust of women that is partly at the root of Marlow's dreadful condition. 'You disgusting tramp!' he screams at Nicola on her first visit to the hospital, 'You two-bit rutting whore! . . . Who are you opening your legs for now you . . . stinking bag of filth . . .' (84). This deeply misogynistic impulse is quickly picked up by Gibbon, who diagnoses Marlow's distorted view of women and sex very early on in his treatment (43–4):

DR GIBBON: You don't like Women. Do you?
MARLOW: Which sort do you mean? Young ones. Old ones. Fat ones. Thin ones. Faithful ones. Slags? Sluts? Try to be more specific.
Gibbon permits himself a grim little smile.
DR GIBBON: All right. Let me rephrase that. I'm reasonably sure that you think you do like them. That you even think they are – well – capable of being idolized, or – You don't like sex. You probably think you do. I mean, we spend a great deal of time thinking about it, don't we?

77

> MARLOW: (*Snarl*) You do. You dirty little sod.
> DR GIBBON: (*Smile*) Yes. I do. But – listen to yourself – isn't it clear that you regard sexual intercourse with considerable distaste – or more to the point, with fear.

As hinted at here, a symptom of Marlow's fear of sex is that he learns to divide women into two distinct types: those who he thinks are sexually predatory and those who he thinks are not. As John Wyver explains, Potter's female characters 'are either angels, before they are seduced (before the Fall), or they are whores' – after their seduction (1992: 20). This 'angel/whore' dichotomy is present in a great deal of Potter's work, but is perhaps most literally dramatised in *Pennies from Heaven* where Eileen sets out (typically enough) as the virgin schoolmistress in the Forest of Dean. 'Never thought I'd see an angel', Arthur sings when he first catches sight of her. However, after her 'Fall' (her seduction) she is banished from 'Eden' and literally forced to live in London as a prostitute called Lulu.

As Potter's career developed so he came to gradually recognise this stereotypical portrayal of women in his own work, acknowledging that his female characters were often not fully rounded figures in their own right, but simply manifestations of his male characters' unconscious fears and desires. He told Graham Fuller that his (almost always male) protagonists 'blame women because that's the source of their unease and their wistfulness and their sexual tension. That's traditional male language. You blame it on the temptress, in religious culture the unclean vessel. But of course it's coming from the man' (cited by Fuller, 1993: 133).

This stereotypical view of women is clearly detectable in *The Singing Detective*. For example, Nicola (a 'two-bit rutting whore') is clearly associated with the colour red – her red nails, hair and clothing perhaps dramatically signifying a 'scarlet woman'. Of course, Mrs Marlow's hair is also red (although a softer shade), implicitly offering a connection between these two 'treacherous' characters. As the story develops, so that connection becomes clearer but it is signalled early on by their tonal similarities. In contrast, the 'angelic' Nurse Mills is always dressed in pale colours, an innocent 'snow white'. Although this is partly because of her hospital uniform, even when she plays the part of the nightclub singer in Marlow's detective story her outfit is very pale blue, perhaps suggesting a purity and innocence that none of the other female characters possess. The way she is shot is also usually brightly lit or in soft focus, while Nicola is generally more associated with shadows and the darkness of Finney's dimly lit apartment.

This split between 'angel' and 'whore' presents specific problems for Potter's male characters. They desire 'angels' but once these innocents have been seduced they are no longer to be trusted. You can detect this sexual neurosis at work in Potter's *Casanova*, where the central protagonist longs for an endless supply of virginal women. However, he is quickly consumed with feelings of disgust and regret after his passion has been satisfied (see Creeber, 1998: 158–66). Potter's

79

Eileen as angel (*Pennies from Heaven*)

Eileen as whore (*Pennies from Heaven*)

male characters frequently deal with this problem by worshipping 'angels' (sometimes referred to, like Nurse Mills, as 'the girl in those songs' [220]), but only having sex with prostitutes or women deemed to be 'tarts'. This may be because, if sex is paid for, then it ceases to become an intimate transaction and becomes primarily an economic one. Consequently, prostitution can also allow a man to retain power over a sexual act that he may unconsciously fear by degrading the woman and abusing her. This may help to explain why Marlow's detective story is filled with prostitutes and why we will later see him visit one in real life. It is a form of sexual intercourse that has little connection with love or tenderness. Of course, the shame he feels for frequenting prostitutes (not exactly in line with his chapel-going background) only adds to the growing sense of guilt that is quite literally crippling him.[28]

Psychoanalysis suggests that such a view of women could

Snow White

originate in the man's inability to enjoy making love with a lover unless she is debased and objectified in some way. His wife, whom he loves and respects, can no longer perform such a function. 'I'm sorry . . .,' explains Marlow to a prostitute he has just slept with, 'It wasn't me calling you names. I don't mean them' (182). As Freud puts it, the 'erotic life of such people remains dissociated, divided between two channels, the same two that are personified in art as heavenly and earthly love. Where such men love they have no desire and where they desire they cannot love' (1954: 207). Such a context certainly helps to explain the way that sex is portrayed in *The Singing Detective* as a whole. As Therese Lichtenstein puts it (1990: 172):

> . . . sexual climax represents a deathlike loss of power, and an intolerable melting of the boundaries between men and women and the frightening figures of women . . . Small wonder that in *The Singing Detective*, sex is

Scarlet woman

never represented as mutually pleasurable for men and women. It is passionless, guilty, often paid for in one way or another, and often related to death and violence.

These passionless and guilty encounters are linked to Marlow's unconscious fear of sex, a fear of intimacy that clearly has its roots in his troubled childhood. Although he is not physically or sexually abused as a child, his witnessing of the sexual act is clearly as influential on his life (and his sexual development) as any case of sexual molestation. The theme of child abuse is certainly one that was often revisited in Potter's work as a whole, children frequently suffering at the hands of an adult's sexual desires (see, for example, *Moonlight on the Highway*).[29] The writer himself suggested that this may have been something that was connected with his own childhood experience (Potter, 1994: 50):

Why-Why-Why? The same desperately repeated question I had asked myself without any sort of answer, or any ability to tell my mother or my father, when, at the age of ten, between VE day and VJ day, I had been trapped by an adult's appetite and abused out of innocence. If anyone cares to look, really look, at my work over the years, they would not take too long to see how the great bulk of it is about the victim, someone who cannot explain, cannot put into the right words, or even cannot speak at all.

The 'abuse' at the centre of *The Singing Detective* is primarily the 'incestuous' relationship between Marlow and his mother. Watching her have sexual intercourse has clearly left a disturbing impression on his mind, one that is played out in various forms in his fiction, fantasies and even his real relationship with his wife. In particular, Marlow's psycho-sexual anxieties appear to reflect aspects of an 'Oedipus Complex'. According to Freud, the traditional paradigm in a (male) child's psychological development is to first select the mother as the object of libidinal interest. However, this is expected to arouse the father's anger, which leads the boy to unconsciously wish for his death, also leaving him the sole benefactor of his mother's affections.

   This Oedipal impulse can be found in a number of Potter plays and serials, not least an early single drama called *Schmoedipus* (BBC, 1974), later reworked into the film *Track 29* directed by Nicolas Roeg and staring Gary Oldman. Indeed, the very title of the original play is an explicit reference to Freud's theory, coming from a joke about a Jewish mother who takes her son to see a psychiatrist. When told he is suffering from an Oedipus Complex she replies, 'Oedipus, Schmoedipus, what does it matter so long as the boy loves his mother?' In both play and film a young man turns up at a suburban home claiming to be the long lost son of a middle-aged housewife. Although now in his early twenties he behaves like a small child, urging his 'mother' to read him bedtime stories and play childish games. 'I spy with my little eye,' he declares, 'something beginning with – "B",' his hand reaching provocatively towards her breasts. 'Did you ever feed me?' he asks her, his mouth resting suggestively near a nipple. Although

for *Track 29* the setting was changed from Britain to America, much of
the original story (including its Oedipal themes) remained, John
Lennon's heart-wrenching song 'Mother' signalling the young man's
arrival at the maternal home.

Such Oedipal desires may be normal in early childhood (Freud
argues that it is how the 'Super-Ego' comes into being), but to display
such an impulse in adulthood does suggest a form of sexual neurosis.
Those individuals who do not develop normally through the Oedipal
phase can later play out its psycho-drama in various displaced,
abnormal and exaggerated ways; particularly if normal sexual
relationships are not developed successfully in later life. As the
psychologist Otto Fenichel puts it, '[w]hen the adult person later
experiences sexual disappointment, he tends to fall back to infantile
sexuality. The result is that the conflicts that raged about his sexuality in
childhood likewise become mobilised again'(1966: 57).

We can certainly detect an Oedipal impulse in *The Singing*

84

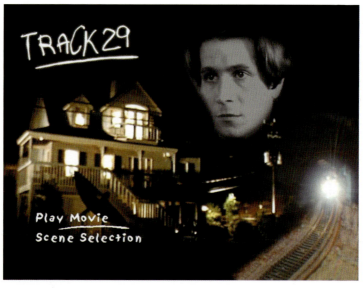

Track 29

Detective. Because of what Marlow secretly sees in the forest he is implicitly connected sexually with his mother and he also rejects his father by becoming emotionally distant from him. This is perhaps why the serial is sometimes compared with Shakespeare's *Hamlet*, which Freud famously argued shares a similar Oedipal structure (see Cook, 1998: 230–1). As Nancy Banks-Smith put it, 'it is demonstrably Potter's *Hamlet*: the wanton mother, the betrayed father, even the built in detective story' (cited by Hunningher, 1993: 254). I would also add Alfred Hitchcock's *Psycho* (1960) to this Oedipal comparison. The last scene of the film shows Norman Bates (Anthony Perkins) in a prison cell, his mind completely dominated by the persona of his dead mother. This is not the only similarity that Potter shared with Hitchcock, as John Caughie explains: both display an 'obsessive mixture of guilt and redemption, repression and excess, sexual fear and sexual aggression . . .' (2000: 176). Interestingly, the mother's house in *Track 29* bears an

Psycho

85

uncanny similarity to the Bates' family home, a subtle indication perhaps of their related themes.

In particular, *The Singing Detective* seems to reveal a recurring interest in motherhood as a whole, a concern that is usually coded in subtle but discernibly sexual terms. For example, in the hospital the elderly George is repeatedly asked the name of his wife by a doctor. However, he seems unable to recall it or even able to understand the question. Finally, he replies, 'Mum. I call her Mum' (73). Minutes later we catch our first glimpse of the primal scene, but instead of Mrs Marlow on her back with Binney it is Nicola. 'Phil-ip!' she cries. '... Why don't you join us' (75). 'My babby. My babby' (115) Raymond will later cry when making love to Mrs Marlow, a role reversal that still implicitly emphasises incestuous sexuality. Interestingly, when Mark Binney first meets the detective he swears on his 'mother's life' that nothing 'nasty' happened to Sonia while she was with him. But Marlow disagrees, arguing that '... [s]omething nasty did happen to her. Wouldn't that be the way that her mother would see it?' 'Her *mother*,' Binney seems bemused, 'for God sake' (62).

Linked to the Oedipus Complex is Freud's notion of the castration complex. According to Freud, the unconscious fear of castration usually begins with the discovery of genital difference in childhood. When seeing female genitalia (typically the mother's) for the first time, a boy will falsely assume that she has had her penis removed, probably as punishment for some misbehaviour. The boy then becomes anxious that the same might happen to him, becoming particularly concerned that his father will castrate him when he discovers the boy's true feelings for his mother. The female genitals also hold a particular threat to the male child as they may appear invisible or mutilated, threatening to engulf and remove his own penis.

There is certainly a proliferation of dangerous-looking 'holes' in *The Singing Detective*. The hospital, the steam train and the underground all have their own dark tunnels and corridors. 'They were sitting on the wooden seats near the end of the [underground] platform,' states the script, 'where the black hole gapes' (184). When George dies in the hospital bed next to Marlow it is a discussion about the easy availability of women at the end of World War II that seems to bring about his cardiac arrest. 'They'd come out of *holes*, these krauts, wouldn't they? Holes in the grahnd,' he tells Marlow, '. . . couple of fags it was for a shag' (emphasis in the original: 109). Instead of calling for help as the man begins to struggle for breath, Marlow viciously presses him on his story. 'Are they coming out of their holes in the ground, George?' he torments him. '[A]ll those helpless little blonde girls with frightened eyes' (ibid.). Moments later we witness the forest scene for the first time.

As Vernon W. Gras points out, not only are the majority of the songs in the drama about women and sex but the records themselves are also explicitly connected with female genitalia (Gras, 2000: 98–104). 'Look at the hole,' his Granddad (Wally Thomas) tells Philip as the record goes round on the turntable. 'That's right,' his uncle (Ken Stott) says crudely with a wink. 'Always keep your eyes on the hole' (128). Rick Wallach (2000) even detects Potter's obsession with another type of 'hole' altogether in his discussion of sodomy and excrement in his revealing and original analysis of *Lipstick on Your Collar* (C4, 1993).

Such references are alluded to in the opening few minutes of *The Singing Detective*. 'And so the man went down the hole like Alice,' narrates our detective. 'But there were no bunny rabbits down there. It was not that sort of hole. It was a rat-hole' (2). This reference to *Alice in Wonderland* (1865) (Alice falls down a hole at the beginning of the story and meets a talking rabbit) is not unusual in Potter's work. He even explored the life of its writer Lewis Carroll in an early single play called *Alice* (BBC, 1965), later reworked into the film *Dreamchild* (Millar, 1985); the theme of sexual abuse clearly apparent in both. As Potter told Fuller, 'I was interested in the fictive Alice but I was also interested in the troubled Dodgson [Carroll's real name] character – the fact that Alice's mother tore up his letters. That haunted soul, who didn't stutter when talking to little girls but was done for as soon as they reached puberty' (cited by Fuller, 1993: 119).

Tunnel vision

Marlow's early mention of a 'rat-hole' might also be significant because it could conjure up associations with one of Freud's most famous case studies, the 'Rat Man'. This patient developed castration anxieties in childhood because his father severely reprimanded him for displaying early sexual curiosity. According to Freud, unconscious anger was therefore directed at his father (and others who were close to him) and he became obsessed with the fact that they would be eaten by rats. While it is a complex and controversial case study, the main conclusion that Freud came to was that the man's obsession with rats was believed to keep him from making difficult decisions in his current life, to ward off the anxiety that would be involved in directly experiencing his angry and aggressive impulses. Keeping in mind the general perception of the rat as a *dirty* animal, it would certainly suggest that a 'rat-hole' is rich with sexual overtones for Marlow.

Marlow's fear of intimacy and his tendency to hide himself in his own fantasy world also culminate in him repeating the voyeuristic position he once adopted in the forest. Notice even when Binney has sex with Sonia that he looks into the mirror (with some disgust) rather than at her, his objectification of her reflected by his apparent detachment from the act itself. Rather than participate in life, Marlow appears to exclude himself from the world and simply becomes a perpetual observer; his illness and voyeuristic tendencies perhaps an unconscious means of retreating from intimacy. In a now classic article, Geraldine Pederson-Krag argues that the detective story represents the curious child who seeks to ferret out the secrets of grown-up sexuality, that is, the 'crime' he or she aims to unravel is the primal scene. As such, the reader of a detective story adopts a quintessentially voyeuristic position towards the 'crime', able to enjoy the investigation but without any fear of reprisal or punishment. As she puts it (Pederson-Krag, 1976: 62):

89

> The voyeur is never entirely satisfied with his peeping which he has the compulsion endlessly to repeat like the detective story addict who re-reads the same basic mystery tale without tedium. In the gradual revelation of

clues that make up the bulk of the narrative, the reader is presented with one significant detail after another, a protracted visual forepleasure. Finally the crime is reconstructed, the mystery solved, that is, the primal scene is exposed. The reader has no need to take part in this by directly identifying with the characters because the gratification is obtained from being a passive onlooker.

As this suggests, Marlow's sexual psychology is a complex and ambiguous terrain. As viewers we are not perhaps meant to uncover or appreciate every Freudian connotation or complex, but what is important is that we begin to make the connections between Marlow's fantasy life and his distorted and perverse view of women and sex. Although Potter's work was often criticised by feminists for its portrayal of women, *The Singing Detective* is ultimately a critique and deconstruction of patriarchal desire and the kind of art that it has traditionally produced. In particular, it interrogates the stereotypical portrayal of women that sees the female figure simply as representative of male fears and desires – thereby denying women their own humanity.[30]

What Marlow discovers during his time in hospital is that his world has been determined by deeply misogynistic impulses that are embedded in his culture, but also his own psycho-sexual origins and development. In particular, his understanding of women is linked with his mother, a formative and overwhelming influence that will forever taint his view of, and relationships with, the opposite sex. Only by deconstructing his psycho-sexual development will Marlow ever truly be free of the psychological anxieties that are at the root of the condition that imprisons him. This is Marlow's real journey, one that will eventually force him to face up to his own unconscious fear of women and sex. His detective story and his childhood songs will reveal this to him, for they are eventually the keys that will gradually unlock the doors of his troubled unconscious.

5 Stories, Songs, Discourse

The darkness that fills the mirror of the past, which lurks in a dark corner or obscures a dark passage out of the oppressively dark city, is not merely the key adjective of so many *film noir* titles but the obvious metaphor for the condition of the protagonist's mind.

Alain Silver and Elizabeth Ward (1980: 36)

Understanding Marlow's sexual psychology a little more means that we can begin to see how it is reflected and articulated in his fantasies, fiction and even the popular songs from his childhood. The way that his fantasy life both constructs and reflects his dysfunctional view of the world is one of the central themes of the serial, offering an exploration into the notion of identity that touches upon issues of discourse, realism and truth. Marlow's fictions and fantasies become a site of his repressed desires and frustrations, a 'text' that is filled with his unconscious anxieties and complex neurosis. By 'rewriting' his detective story he slowly begins to uncover aspects of himself that he did not know existed. What he discovers is a shadowy world of metaphor and symbolism that appears to reveal a great deal that is perhaps too painful for its author to confront directly.

It is perhaps an obvious point to make, but Philip Marlow is a hugely frustrated man. In terms of relationships, he has only one visitor while in hospital: an estranged wife whom he abuses and distrusts. Although an author, his novel 'The Singing Detective' is not only out of print but its genre is generally looked down upon by critics, who tend to deem it as 'pulp', 'trash' or what Gibbon calls 'cheap literature' (51). His written work certainly does not seem to have made him either famous or wealthy (he jokes that his only assets are his Reader's Digest prize draws). He also suffers from a profound sexual frustration, as Nurse Mills discovers to her cost. In short, Marlow seems to have led a disappointing life. 'I used to think', he tells Ali (Badi Uzzaman), 'I wanted the good opinion of honourable men and the ungrudging love of beautiful women . . . But now I know *for sure* that all I really want is a cigarette' (13). It is perhaps for these reasons that he turns in on himself, making his fantasy life so rich and compelling. According to Freud, this is not a rare occurrence for the creative individual (Freud, 1976: 423):

> An artist is once more in rudiments an introvert, not far removed from
> neurosis. He [sic] is oppressed by excessively powerful instinctual needs.
> He desires to win honour, power, wealth, fame and the love of women; but
> lacks the means for achieving these satisfactions. Consequently, like any
> other unsatisfied man, he turns away from reality and transfers all his
> interest and his libido too, to the wishful constructions of his life of
> phantasy . . .

It is these frustrations that we can find in all aspects of Marlow's life, but particularly the imaginary world he constructs around himself. Marlow's detective story, for example, is a text around which many of his frustrated desires are unconsciously expressed. The actual detective plot (which involves some form of espionage with both Russian and former Nazi agents) is arguably unimportant compared to its dramatisation of Marlow's unconscious anxieties. In fact, its lack of importance might be seen as one of the weaknesses of the serial as a whole; the detective story gradually losing its meaning and slowly merging into Marlow's paranoid delusions about his wife and the

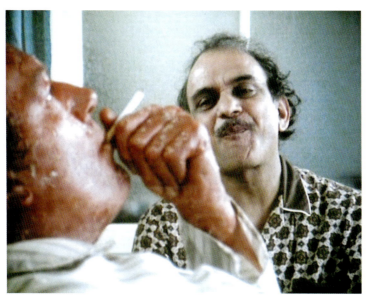

'All I really want is a cigarette'

93

stolen screenplay as the serial progresses. However, what is important is the *way* the detective story is being told and what this tells us about its author's psychological condition. It is the connections made between Marlow's life and his art that are really under examination here.

Marlow's detective story reflects the work of writers like Dashiell Hammett and Raymond Chandler. This genre of literature went on to inform film noir with many of Hammett and Chandler's novels being adapted for the big screen. With its roots in German Expressionist cinematography, film noir (simply French for 'black film') was defined by its dark, dramatic lighting and the subjective, psychological point of view of its characters – characters that are often imprisoned in a seemingly nihilistic and existentially pessimistic world. In particular, the stories told of people trapped in situations that were generally not of their own making, striving against random and uncaring fate. It is no accident, then, that Potter chose film noir as the means to dramatise Marlow's psychological anxieties; the genre subtly reflecting his own dark, pessimistic and alienated view of the world.

The figure of the detective is often taken to be one of the defining features of film noir. This hard-boiled detective has become particularly associated with the actor Humphrey Bogart, whose performances as Hammett's Sam Spade in *The Maltese Falcon* (Huston, 1941) and as Chandler's Philip Marlowe in *The Big Sleep* (Hawks, 1946) established him as the iconic private eye. Bogart was particularly important in creating the feel of these movies – a hard-drinking, hard-loving, fast-talking male hero for an increasingly dangerous world. In particular, Bogart portrayed an unsentimental and cynical man, but one who still embodied and lived by a form of common and everyday decency. As Chandler famously put it in *The Simple Art of Murder* (1988: 18):

> He is a relatively poor man, or he would not be a detective at all. He is a
> common man or he could not go among common people. He has a sense of
> character, or he would not know his job. He will take no man's dishonesty
> and no man's insolence without a due and dispassionate revenge. He is a
> lonely man and his pride is that you will treat him as a proud man or be very
> sorry you ever saw him. He talks as the man of his age talks – that is, with
> rude wit, a lively sense of the grotesque, a disgust for sham, and a contempt
> for pettiness. . . . If there were enough like him, the world would be a very
> safe place to live in, without becoming too dull to be worth living in.

Not surprisingly, Bogart's incarnation of the hard-boiled detective has since become synonymous with a jaded and unemotional form of masculinity. As John Cawelti explains, the detective's 'price of survival would seem to be a terrible emptiness, a restriction of human possibilities, a cynical rejection of deeper emotion and commitment . . . Only a rejection of all emotional and moral ties can help a man survive in this treacherous world' (1976: 167–8). Consequently, the iconic figure of Bogart offers a stark contrast to how men have changed since the arrival of feminism in the 1960s and 1970s. In particular, the figure of Bogart has often being used in contemporary culture to symbolise something men may have lost in their post-war 'feminisation'. You can clearly detect this in a film like *Dead Men Don't Wear Plaid* (Reiner, 1982), where old detective movies (including Bogart's *The Big Sleep*, *In a Lonely Place* [Ray, 1950] and *Dark Passage* [Daves, 1947]) are edited together with new material to produce an ironic spoof of the genre, particularly satirising Bogart's self-assured masculine bravado. Steve Martin (who appeared as Arthur in the film version of *Pennies from Heaven*) plays Rigby Reardon, a low-life gumshoe. 'It was a street of frustrated hopes and broken dreams,' he narrates, 'everything was cheap, cut-rate. Even the prostitutes were having a sale.'

The iconic figure of Bogart was also employed in Woody Allen's *Play it Again, Sam* (1972) (directed by Herbert Ross, the director of the film version of *Pennies from Heaven*), its title coming from the famously misquoted line from Bogart in *Casablanca* (Curtiz, 1942).[31] Indeed, Allen's alter ego comes in the 'real' shape of a Bogart look-a-like (Jerry Lacy) who guides Allen's neurotic protagonist in his inept pursuit of women. It is a strikingly similar technique to the one Potter employs, the anxious and insecure contemporary male finding expression and courage in the archetypal hard-boiled detective. As Allen fusses and stresses over his chat-up lines and his need to please a woman, 'Bogart' tells him bluntly how to deal with the opposite sex. 'There's no secret, kid,' he explains. 'Dames are simple. I've never known one that doesn't understand a slap in the mouth or a slug from a 45.'

Like Allen's 'Bogart', Marlow's hard-boiled 'alter ego' is everything the hospital patient is not. The private eye, complete with raincoat and 'mid-Atlantic, little side-of-the-mouth quips' (100), is tough, macho, healthy and streetwise. Like the real Marlow, this private eye has difficulty understanding or 'getting in touch' with his emotions. 'I can sing the singing,' he explains, 'I can think the thinking ... But you're not going to catch me feeling the feeling. No sir' (86). But unlike the real Marlow he is not forced to do so by a persistent psychiatrist. This is perhaps why Marlow feels so secure in this fictional world, a

Play it Again, Sam

landscape strictly controlled by rigid narrative conventions rather than real and uncontrollable emotions.[32] 'OK. OK. So what's the story? Who's the dame?' his alter ego asks Binney. When Binney enquires how he knows there is a woman involved he replies, '[t]here's always a dame . . . There's always a body, too. I know that. You know that' (50).

As this suggests, this hard-boiled world of the detective has strict generic guidelines, particularly when it comes to the role of 'dames'. In particular, feminist film critics have argued that film noir tends to reduce all women to one of two roles – the virgin and the femme fatale. The virgin in such films is usually passive, sexually naive and subservient to men, while the femme fatale is openly sexual, active and a threat to male power. As Janey Place explains, film noir 'is a male fantasy, as is most of our art. Thus woman here as elsewhere is defined by her sexuality: the dark lady has access to it and the virgin does not' (1986: 35). The 'dark lady' must therefore be punished for her sexual and social transgressions, usually paying with her life for tempting the man away from traditional modes of behaviour. As women during the war period were given new-found independence and better job-earning power, critics have argued that they therefore had to suffer on the screen (the 'dark lady' representing the modern, independent woman that traditional men unconsciously feared).

It is this generic portrayal of women that makes the film noir tradition such an ideal vehicle through which we are allowed to view Marlow's own psychological relationship with the opposite sex. In particular, its tendency to split women into 'virgins' or 'femme fatales' perfectly mirrors Marlow's own tendency to divide women into 'angels' and 'whores'. His psychological make-up has clearly attracted him to the genre and allowed him to dramatise his unconscious anxieties around women and sex. This helps to explain the number of prostitutes and duplicitous women in his story, reflecting a sinister, menacing and misogynistic world view. Seen in this light, the detective story is simply the fictional representation of Marlow's own deep-rooted fears and desires.

Take, for example, Binney's encounter with Sonia, the Russian prostitute/spy and archetypal femme fatale. She is clearly sexually assertive, taking off her fur coat to reveal that she only has underwear on underneath ('the flimsiest, frilliest, most alluring kind' [47]). He gives her money for sex – money that she promptly puts in her mouth, chews and then bizarrely spits onto the floor while laughing in his face. As this suggests, she is a wanton, unpredictable and sexualised female who cares little for social or sexual convention and is clearly not to be trusted. He is therefore intimidated but is also strangely aroused by her, particularly perhaps his need to punish her for her transgressions. 'Binney,' the scripts explains, 'a wholly nasty creature, suddenly slaps her face, in a way that shows he finds exciting' (47). Inevitably, Sonia is murdered after having sex with him, ending up like Mrs Marlow, floating in the River Thames. This, then, is a fictional re-enactment of the sexualised violence that Marlow feels towards women generally, Binney (Marlow's 'id') playing out his unconscious urges while the detective acts as a strongly moral force (Marlow's 'ego').

Some critics have even connected film noir with particular elements of the Oedipus Complex. According to Alenka Zupancic (Zupancic, 2000: 245–6):

> that which brings the story of Oedipus close to the *noir* universe is, of course, the fact that the hero – the detective – is without knowing it, implicated in the crimes he is investigating. One could even say that the story of Oedipus lies at the heart of the "new wave" of *film noir* – films such as *Angel Heart* and *Blade Runner* (the director's cut), where it emerges at the end that the hero is himself the criminal he is looking for.

This connection with *The Singing Detective* is made even more explicit in Mark Fisher's article on *Batman Begins* (Nolan, 2005). As Fisher puts it, its 'hard-bitten world reminds me not so much of *noir*, but of the simulation of *noir* in Dennis Potter's [sic] *Singing Detective*, the daydream-fantasies of a cheap hack, thick with misogyny and misanthropy and cooked in intense self-loathing' (Fisher, 2006).

Indeed, the *Batman* story has also been connected with a deeply Oedipal structure as a whole, his life dedicated to avenging the death of his parents in a random street robbery. According to Fisher (ibid):

> *Batman Begins* re-binds the becoming-animal with the Oedipal by having Bruce's fear of bats figure as a partial cause of his parents' death. Bruce is at the opera when the sight of bat-like figures on stage drives him to nag his parents until they leave the theatre and are killed.

Fisher even goes so far as to explicitly connect the name of Batman to Freud's famous case study of the 'Rat Man'. Like both Batman and 'Rat-Man', Marlow is guilt-ridden for unconsciously wanting his parents dead and consequently disappears into his own symbolic 'hole' – displacing his deepest fantasies into the dark and dangerous world of film noir. 'Into the rat-hole,' Marlow narrates in the serial's opening few minutes, 'Down, down, down' (2).

Whether explicitly 'Oedipal' or not, the film noir universe

does seem to perfectly represent many of Marlow's unconscious fears and desires. One film that is particularly reminiscent of themes in his story is the classic 'B' movie *Detour* (Ulmer, 1945). With its shadowy black-and-white cinematography, cynical narration ('. . . fate sticks out a leg to trip you'), flashbacks and a classic 'dark lady' ('I was tussling with the most dangerous animal in the world – a woman'), it is arguably one of the blackest noir films ever made. The story revolves around Al Roberts (Tom Neal), a penniless piano-player in a smoky New York nightclub' and his fiancée Sue (Claudia Drake), a singer in a band. 'You're going to make Carnegie yet Al,' she tells him. 'Yeah,' he replies, 'if I don't get arthritis first.' When she leaves for Hollywood he eventually decides to join her and hitchhikes across America. However, on the way he becomes accidentally involved in a death and is eventually blackmailed by Vera (Ann Savage), a dishevelled, drunk, manipulative and sexualised shrill of a woman. He finally kills her by accidentally strangling her with a telephone wire, leaving him to constantly fear for his arrest and never rejoin the love of his life. With its dark and expressionistic images, its existential fatalism, its beautiful virgin and Vera's wild-eyed femme fatale, the film almost defines the genre.

99

Detour begins in flash-forward with Roberts sitting alone in a diner trying to forget the whole sordid mess of his life. A man approaches him and tries to make conversation but he is uninterested. 'My mother', he tells him, 'taught me never to speak to strangers.' Angry and insulted the man puts a dime in the jukebox and Roberts suddenly becomes incensed:

That tune. That *tune*! Why was it always that rotten tune? Following me around, beating in my head, never letting up. Did you ever want to forget something? Did you ever want to cut out a piece of your memory? You can't you know, no matter how hard you try. You can change the scenery, but sooner or later you will get a whiff of perfume or somebody may say a certain phrase or hum something, then you're licked again!

Detour

100

This brief speech brings us neatly to the role of the songs in *The Singing Detective*. What is particularly interesting in a film like *Detour* is the way that popular music is seen to evoke memories in its troubled protagonist in a deeply 'Proustian' manner. Reflecting its fascination with pulp fiction and popular culture generally, film noir was able to imbue 'low culture' with a greater significance than was generally accepted or recognised at the time. It is this aspect of popular culture that Potter also appears to be tapping into; the power of so-called 'cheap' fiction/music to articulate feelings (particularly deeply buried memories) that we might prefer to forget. The music is sugary and syncopated (what Marlow describes as 'banality with a beat' [196]), but it nonetheless forces him out of his desperate state of denial.

This is in stark contrast to the way the songs were used in *Pennies from Heaven*, where they appeared to articulate the hidden wonder of existence, what Potter describes as 'the idea of the world shimmering with another reality' (cited by Fuller, 1993: 86). In *The*

Singing Detective they take on a clearly more ambiguous role, their deceptively innocent refrains now charged with ominous secrets and portentous significance. Taking him unawares, they suddenly force our sick protagonist to confront painful memories and emotions, often located in his childhood (the period they originate from). So while the serial's musical sequences partly reflect the bright and jubilant optimism of the Hollywood musical (perhaps the perfect generic contrast to film noir), they essentially articulate deeply repressed feelings and desires. This is why they are often presented in a dark and absurd manner, their trite optimism betrayed by sinister undertones that ironically articulate emotions that Marlow himself seems unable to express. As Potter put it (cited in ibid.: 87):

> Marlow, sick, trying to reassemble himself, was resisting them [the songs], didn't believe in them, or only believed in them in the way he believed in his cheap thrillers. The songs played the same kind of function as his story, his cheap detective novel, which sneaked up on him and revealed to him how much of his own life was in them; how much of his own misogyny and self-pity and his own inner myth was bound up with this cheap writing.

Potter has clearly chosen the songs for *The Singing Detective* with great care. Nostalgic and corny as many of them may seem now, they also resonate with disturbing accuracy Marlow's troubled psychology. They certainly articulate his sense of denial ('I Get Along Without You Very Well'), confinement ('Don't Fence Me In'), guilt ('You Always Hurt the One You Love'), pessimism ('Into Each Life Some Rain Must Fall'), obsession ('The Very Thought of You'), illness ('I've Got You Under My Skin') and loss ('After You've Gone'). Appropriately enough, many of them centre on sexual betrayal. 'Paper Doll' is particularly menacing with its perception of a one-dimensional woman who is completely under the control of a man ('I'm gonna buy a Paper Doll that I can call my own/A doll that other fellows cannot steal'). The ominous tone of the song is made all the more poignant when we see it sung by Marlow's cuckolded father. It is also more than a little disturbing when sung by

101

the solders on the train who are suggestively eyeing up Philip's mother. 'Blues in the Night' is also suggestive of male power, but this time from a woman's point of view ('A man is a two face/A worrisome thing/Who'll leave you to sing/The blues in the night'). A song like 'Do I Worry?' sums up many of these themes with its subtle mixture of jealousy, anxiety and repression:

> Do I worry 'cause you're stepping out,
> Do I worry 'cause you've got me in doubt
> Though your kisses aren't right, do I give a bag of beans,
> Do I stay home every night, and read my magazines,
> Am I frantic 'cause we've lost the spark,
> Is there panic when it starts turning dark,
> And when evening shadows creep,
> Do I lose any sleep over you?
> Do I worry – you can bet your life I do.

102   Set against Marlow's despair and suffering, the trite optimism of some of the music is affectionately mocked ('Tomorrow is a Lovely Day') or else is used to mock others (as in the use of 'Entry of the Queen of Sheba' to accompany the arrival of the pompous doctors in the first episode). Sometimes they ironically express Marlow's anxious state of mind ('I'm as restless as a willow in a windstorm/I'm as jumpy as a puppet on a string/I'd say that I had spring fever/But I know it isn't spring'). Even when they are not dealing specifically in matters of a sexual or emotional nature, the songs nonetheless force Marlow to delve deep into his repressed memories. The 'Teddy Bears' Picnic' accompanies his painful recollection of his mother's infidelity in the forest ('If you go down to the woods today/You're in for a big surprise') and 'Dry Bones' reflects his feeling of alienation both from his own body and the cold and scientific discourse of the medical staff. 'Dry Bones' also has religious overtones ('Ezekiel cried Dem Bones/Now hear the words of the Lord'), a theme reflected in less obvious numbers like 'Ac-cent-tchu-ate the Positive' with its references to Jonah and the Whale and Noah

'Ac-cent-tchu-ate the Positive'

'Paper Doll'

and the Ark. Even seemingly 'innocuous' songs such as 'Cruising Down the River' take on an ominous significance in light of the role the river plays in the drama, while 'The Rustle of Spring' (an instrumental) could implicitly refer to Mrs Marlow's springtime 'rustle' in the Forest of Dean.

The songs are used throughout *The Singing Detective* in many ways, but it is in the 'lip-synching' hallucinations where they are perhaps most pronounced. The introduction of each hallucination signals a break from the narrative diegesis as characters suddenly begin miming and dancing to music that clearly has no origins in the film's diegetic world. Although the classical Hollywood musical employed the practice of 'lip-synch' as a technical device, here Potter utilises that technical consideration and turns it into an aesthetic choice. In contrast with the traditional Hollywood musical, the obvious disjunction between the actor's voice and the singing voice of the original recordings foregrounds the artificiality of these musical intrusions in a seemingly naturalistic narrative.

Sometimes it is the way that the songs are performed that gives them an added meaning or poignancy. The elderly George lip-synching to 'It Might as Well Be Spring' is particularly moving – his evocation of spring is both ironic and sad, given that he is clearly in the winter of his life (he dies shortly after performing the song). Similarly, the 'Teddy Bears' Picnic' is generally regarded as an innocent and childish musical number, but the way it is shot and performed in the serial heightens its more ambiguous connotations. Marlow's alter ego detective delivers the first lines, lit from below in medium close-up so we have no doubt about its menacing undertones. But also notice the black humour of the sequence, neatly summing up the loss of innocence that the song (at least to a contemporary audience) appears to implicitly capture. In particular, Gambon's extraordinary performance as the psoriatic Marlow walking and singing for the first time, looking like a giant teddy bear as he lifts his large body from leg to leg with his arms bent at the side. The accompaniment of the other patients and staff in the ward on various instruments (Noddy desperately tries to play the triangle) also produces comedic possibilities that only heighten the song's absurd and surreal undertones.

Some critics argue that Potter's 'lip-synching' device is meant to have a 'Brechtian' distancing effect on an audience. According to Timothy Corrigan, the 'musical expression as a technological and lip-synched performance removes human expression from the horror and miseries of the different narratives by abstracting and denaturalizing it' (Corrigan, 1991: 186). However, in the majority of cases the songs also strangely provide a sense of human desire within an often inhuman and dehumanising environment. Far from simply producing a technological and commodified experience, the songs appear to offer Marlow an ambiguous reminder of a now forgotten, more organic world than his hospital imprisonment (see Creeber, 1996). Performed by his mother and father in the working-men's club of his childhood, they seem to bring back memories of a time when the young Philip was still held within the very warm embrace of both family and community. Although syncopated and banal, they are transformed into a Hoggartesque form of 'folk culture' that both mirrors and articulates Marlow's longing for a better and far simpler world.[33]

105

The songs certainly capture the alienation and the horror of Marlow's painful condition, but there is an ambiguity in the way that they are employed that also suggests that they (like his detective story) can articulate his deeply suppressed dreams and desires. Although they are undoubtedly American and commercial in origin, they also seem to offer Marlow the reminder of a purer and more innocent British (working-class) culture that he once enjoyed as a boy. 'The songs,' Marlow tells Nurse Mills, 'the bloody, bloody songs . . . the songs you hear coming up the stair . . . When you are a child' (220). Seen in this light, the music appears to tap into something that the adult Marlow has now lost. Although they annoy him with their uncanny ability to get stuck in his head, they constantly remind him of a world that is now out of his grasp – perhaps even a spiritual realm that he has not experienced since he was young (before the forest Fall). Indeed, Potter likened the music in *Pennies from Heaven* to the Psalms of David. 'There's a huge gap, obviously,' he told Graham Fuller, 'between the psalms and those songs, but their function is not dissimilar. It's the idea of the world shimmering with another reality . . .' (cited by Fuller, 1993: 86). Although the music is often made to appear more menacing in *The Singing Detective* than in *Pennies from Heaven*, it still sometimes provides Marlow with something authentically meaningful – an insight into his troubled past and possibly the roots of his neurosis.

In this way, Marlow 'rewrites' the songs of his childhood as he 'rewrites' his detective novel, giving them personal meaning and significance that he had not previously realised. As Potter has put it, they 'are genuine artefacts I'm picking up but it's not serendipity. You're picking them up in order to use them, so it's part of the drama, as though you'd written the tune yourself' (cited in ibid.: 91). It is a transformation of culture and art which suggests that an act of personal revision is also unconsciously taking place. It is not just the songs that Marlow rewrites but, perhaps implicitly, the story of his own life. In order to understand how this is done we need to first appreciate the role of language and storytelling in Marlow's world, a landscape that appears to be defined by a number of competing stories, genres and discourses. As Antony Hilfer puts it (2000: 133–4):

> In *The Singing Detective*, Potter plays off against each other the artistic genres of hard-boiled detective fiction, crime fiction, children's story, and popular music, as well as several discursive genres: medical, psychoanalytic and religious discourse. Each genre implies an alternative ethos to the other genres while simultaneously being qualified by them. Such collisions dramatise competing generic paradigms that imply competing ethical conventions and intuitions. The competing genres shape a story not only produced by generic conventions but also 'about' how stories are produced by generic conventions.

As this suggests, *The Singing Detective* is partly about the functions that stories perform for us; it unravels the significance and construction of narrative and language in our everyday lives. The power of language is something that appears to strike Marlow particularly intensely when he gradually recovers the use of his hands and is able to write again (clearly an important moment for anyone but perhaps even more so for someone who makes their living through writing). He is certainly intoxicated by the beauty of the shapes he is now able to painfully scrawl across the page. 'What's the loveliest word in the English language?' he asks Nurse Mills. 'The sound it makes in your mouth, and the shape it makes on the page' (237). However, Marlow also seems startled by the incredible power of language to manipulate and distort the world around him, particularly its ability to deceive him into saying things he may not mean, as this encounter with his bemused physiotherapist (Tricia George) suggests (226):

MARLOW: . . . Words. Words make me hold my breath.
PHYSIOTHERAPIST: I see.
MARLOW: Who knows what you are going to say? Who knows where they've been?

107

PHYSIOTHERAPIST: Well. Keep at it. You're doing very well.
He can see that she has no idea what he is talking about.
MARLOW: Suppose they get together, and ganged up on us when we weren't looking?
PHYSIOTHERAPIST: Who?
MARLOW: Words. The little devils. *Words.*
She looks at him, then looks at her watch.
PHYSIOTHERAPIST: Well – I'll pop in and see you some time tomorrow afternoon –
MARLOW: Who made you say that?
PHYSIOTHERAPIST: What do you mean?
He stares at her, goes to say something, and changes it as he speaks, with a slightly puzzled air.
MARLOW: . . . No. It doesn't matter. Doesn't matter.

For Marlow, words have an enormous power and can 'gang up' on us, forcing us to see the world in their particular light. While they are clearly 'beautiful' in their own right, we never know whose discourse we are adopting by choosing particular sentences ('Who knows where they've been?'). We seemingly have the freedom to say anything we like, but do we? What makes us choose certain words and how do they change what we perceive and how we are perceived by others? Language helps to articulate our reality, it gives us the power of thought and the ability to make sense of the world, but it also determines who we are and how we act.

Such a perspective may be best understood in the light of post-structuralist accounts of language and discourse. Rather than simply and innocently reflecting the real world, many contemporary critics now argue that language actually *constructs* our view of ourselves and our notions of reality. In particular, we may adopt different 'discourses' that help create and order meaning but, in doing so, artificially frame our world and make us understand it and ourselves through a specific ideological perspective. These 'discourses' (sometimes referred to as 'linguistic genres') can take many forms, for example, religious, historical, philosophical, scientific, political, medical, sexual and psychological. Although they appear to offer us a transparent 'truth' about the world, they are never really anything but *mediators* of reality, linguistic metaphors that are always constructing and determining our view of 'the real'. As Ellen Seiter puts it, 'Discourse is not "free speech". It is not a perfect expression of the speaker's intention. Indeed, we cannot think of communicative intentions as predating the constraints of language at all' (1992: 62).

For example, any account of history purports to offer us a real, authentic and accurate view of the past. However, any description of the past is subject to bias and manipulation. It is not the truth but a linguistic representation of past events and so ultimately another 'story'. Although religious texts try to avoid such criticism by arguing that they were written by great prophets or God and are therefore beyond such questioning, they too could be seen as simply another story. In this sense, religious texts are open to revision like any other, their meanings are not absolute but always subject to reinterpretation by new readers who may contest or revise previous accounts. This theoretical perspective is even acknowledged in the introduction of a recent edition of *The Bible: The Authorized King James Version*, which argues that (Carroll and Prickett, 1997: xiv):

> far from representing an objective and complete viewpoint, all 'history' consists of narratives written by particular people, with particular opinions and experiences, at particular moments in time – and that includes, of course, this definition of history under discussion. Similarly, no readers can imagine they approach the Bible (or any other text) from an objective or absolute standpoint. Each can only come to it from a particular standpoint and perspective. Particularity is a condition of knowledge. In that respect 'history' is the word we use to describe a particular kind, or genre, of narrative writing.

Marlow perhaps first discovers this insight into the power of language and discourse when he stands up in front of his classmates and blames another boy for something he has done. What he witnesses then is how his story slowly gets collaborated by the rest of the children and gradually solidifies into a 'truth'. 'Interestingly –', he tells Gibbon, 'what is interesting – the boy was *himself* overwhelmed by the weight of the evidence . . . And this poor little sod came in the end to believe that he *had* done it . . .' (212–13). As a result, Marlow's first exercise in public storytelling ends up with him inventing a lie that everyone eventually comes to accept, even the very boy who suffered from it the most. 'I sat in my desk, perjurer, charlatan,' he tells Gibbon, 'and watched and listened and watched and listened as one after another they nailed that backward lad hands and feet to my story' (212). In this sense, we are all crucified by language and the power of stories, whether they are actually true or not.

There are certainly many different languages or discourses in *The Singing Detective*, constantly pushing and pulling our hero in different directions as he desperately tries to make sense of his fractured world. As we have seen, Marlow employs the 'hard-boiled' language of the American detective story to protect himself and to hide his emotions, but there is also the medical discourse of the hospital staff that conceives his illness purely and coldly in scientific terms ('Librium', 'Valium', 'Antidepressants' [28]) and the religious discourse which dictates much of Marlow's personal universe. Indeed, the Bible is one of the first narratives ('The Greatest Story Ever Told') that Philip learns and one that (particularly its notion of original sin) will have a huge influence on how he will learn to interpret and make sense of his own life. There is also the 'discourse' of psychoanalysis that helps Marlow to reorder and make sense of his past. The storytelling nature of psychoanalysis is evident in the description of it as 'the talking cure' in which a patient (the analysand) tells their story to the analyst, who then interprets and shapes it much like a text. Although Marlow is clearly helped in his recovery by therapy, his hostile and cynical approach to it (and his psychiatrist) may not only be the fear of what it might uncover, but also the awareness that it is ultimately yet another 'story'.

This is a notion of psychoanalysis that is all too apparent to feminist critics of Freud, who describe his language and ideas as inherently sexist. For example, Freud's notion of 'penis envy' suggests that all young girls see their vagina as inferior to a boy's penis, regarding it as a negative attribute rather than a positive one. Such a theory places the woman as lacking something that the man has, thereby casting her as 'Other', while the male is established as the norm (perhaps reflecting an Old Testament view of gender). So if we were to take Freudian discourse at face value we might be in danger of allowing its biased construction of gender to distort our view of the world (see Zoonen, 1994: 22). While psychoanalysis is clearly useful to Marlow, its discourse can never escape the limitations by which all stories are contained. This may even help explain Potter's decision to call his psychiatrist Dr Gibbon, perhaps an implicit reference to the scientific discourse of evolution that could be seen to reduce all humanity to the level of apes and monkeys.[34]

'The talking cure'

This conception of language and discourse might even explain one of the most controversial aspects of the serial, Marlow's ambiguous relationship with his Asian bedfellow, Ali. On first glance, his language to Ali appears decidedly racist, calling him 'nig-nog' and complaining to Dr Finlay about 'immigrants' (11). However, while entering into the 'discourse' of racism, his fondness for Ali is also abundantly clear. The script insists that there 'is obviously an affection between them' (12) and Marlow's jibes seem to be done with a great deal of humour and a genuine warmth. 'One thing about this place,' he tells his friend, 'it strips away all the important stuff – like skin' (13). Indeed, one of the most moving moments of the first episode comes when Marlow sucks on one of Ali's precious sweets after he has died; tears flowing down his cracked face.

Ironically, Ali appears more comfortable with Marlow's affectionately 'racist' remarks than he is with the professional and patronising discourse of the earnest doctors. Through a mixture of poor English and an abject fear of authority, Ali unintentionally frustrates Dr Finlay by not actually understanding his attempt to help (14):

> DR FINLAY: Are you having trouble with this fellow?
> ALI: (*Beam*) Oh yes, my God yes.
> DR FINLAY: Has he been making offensive remarks about your origins?
> ALI: (*Puzzled*) Origins?
> DR FINLAY: Your – ah – race, or – ?
> ALI: Race?
> DR FINLAY: (*Irritated*) Yes. Your race!
> MARLOW: Go on. Tell him. You brown bugger.
> *Ali gives a whoop of laughter. Dr Finlay, taken aback, goes to say something but – bleep-bleep-bleep! goes his bleeper, and he turns on his heels to stride away, angrily frustrated.*

112 As this suggests, *The Singing Detective* is fundamentally about the ability of language and discourse to both reveal and conceal the world around us. Words are not to be trusted and neither are the stories that they tell, they distort and manipulate reality rather than innocently reflect it – they sometimes even mean the exact opposite of what is actually said or written. As Hilfer points out (2000: 137), when Gibbon plays the word-association game with his patient, Marlow responds to 'sentence' with 'prison', perhaps reflecting the inability of escaping from 'the prison house of language' (see Jameson, 1972). Rather than allowing us to see the world freely, language and discourse confines and imprisons us in its rigid rules and conventions.

In this sense, Marlow's detective novel perhaps contains as much truth about himself as his own memories and recollections. Both are linguistic 'versions' of the past and both involve elements of 'fact' and 'fantasy'. The serial's constant blurring of different generic worlds implicitly suggests as much, thus presenting an inherently intertextual universe where the boundaries between the 'real' and 'fantasy' have

Shadows

broken down. Perhaps this explains the drama's obsession with shadows, tunnels and darkened rooms. Notice, for example, Nicola's shadow play on the wall of Finney's dimly lit apartment; her childish game perhaps suggestive of a world we can only know through deceptive reflections and blurry silhouettes (a theme implicitly dramatised by film noir).

These are questions about language and discourse that occupied much of Potter's drama as a whole. In *Follow the Yellow Brick Road* (BBC, 1972), Jack Black (Denholm Elliot) believes that his life is being written by a TV dramatist – which, ironically, it is (as we discover at its end when the machinery of the TV studio is suddenly revealed). Similarly, in *Double Dare* (BBC, 1976) a dramatist overhears dialogue he has written coming out of the mouths of apparently 'real' people around him. The same device is also employed in the posthumous *Karaoke*, a serial whose very title implies the notion of a world in which people simply 'mouth' the words of others. Just as Potter's characters famously 'lip-synch' to pre-recorded songs, so 'karaoke culture' suggests a world where, rather than us simply speaking language, language speaks us.

As this suggests, *The Singing Detective* can partly be seen as an attempt to reveal the complexities of the stories we construct around ourselves so that their essentially artificial nature can be exposed and interrogated. This gives us an insight into Potter's work as a whole which, as we have seen, rarely tried to represent the 'real' world but attempted (through 'anti-realist' or 'non-naturalistic' techniques) to do justice to the inner psychology and subjective realities of life in all its narrative twists and generic ambiguities. As Potter put it (Potter, 1977; also cited by Caughie, 2000: 152):

> Most television ends up offering its viewers a means of orientating themselves towards the generally received notions of 'reality'. . . . The best non-naturalistic drama, in its very structure, disorientates the viewer smack in the middle of the orientation process which television perpetually uses. It disrupts the patterns that are endemic to television, and upsets or exposes the narrative styles of so many of the other allegedly non-fiction programmes. It shows the frame in the picture when most television is showing the picture in the frame.

What Potter seems to be suggesting here is that because realism refuses to reveal its artificiality ('the picture in the frame'), it fails to acknowledge and accept that it is little more than a 'story' (i.e. a particular *version* of the world). Ironically, it is only by accepting the limitations of storytelling that a narrative can ever get near to grasping the 'truth' about the world. Stories must contain within them the power to be open, otherwise they become a 'prison-house' through which we no longer innocently recognise the world but have the world *written* for us. Many of these issues are alluded to in a conversation Nicola has with Marlow in hospital. 'Write about real things in a realistic way,' she insists, '– real people, real joys, real pains – not these silly detective stories. Something more relevant' (140). For Marlow, however, any form of fiction that purports to represent the real is doomed to *mis*represent it, simply because reality is always more complex and open-ended than these 'real' fictions can ever convey. 'All solutions, and no clues,' Marlow tells her. 'That's what the dumb-heads want. That's the bloody Novel – He said, she said, and descriptions of the sky – I'd rather it was the other way around. All clues. No solutions. That's the way things are. Plenty of clues. No solutions' (ibid.).

Potter's interest in the differences between 'realism' and 'non-naturalism' may date back to the time of an early documentary he made about the Forest of Dean called *Between Two Rivers* (BBC, 1960). To his dismay, he felt that the programme had belittled the people of the forest and that its documentary realism had failed to adequately reflect or articulate the truth about his beloved community. He subsequently felt a strong sense of guilt about the programme as a whole, feeling he had patronised his birth-place and had used and manipulated its people (see Creeber, 1998a: 42–7). He would later argue that this is one of the reasons that he felt so compelled to turn his back on realist or documentary techniques as a whole, sensing that the very playfulness and artificiality of drama (particularly in its non-naturalistic form) could not simplify or reduce the complexity or ambiguity of the world in quite the same way. According to Potter, it 'taught me how easy the betrayal is compared to, using the word in quotes if you like, "art", which is not concerned with betrayal, and art cannot betray in that sense' (Potter, 1994: 63). Notice the use of the word 'betrayal' here – an almost biblical act of treachery against his birth-place that appears to equal Marlow's own betrayal of his family and community.

In contrast, by heightening the generic conditions and complexities of Marlow's story *The Singing Detective* implicitly asks its audience to question the 'stories' that are all too frequently mistaken for the truth. In doing so, it ironically aims to give its audiences the 'truth' by drawing their attention to its artificial and constructed form. Realism may think it is representing the real, but it is actually distorting it by refusing to accept and acknowledge its narrative limitations; offering neat solutions and conclusions to the impenetrable ambiguities of real life. All genres may attempt to reflect 'the real' but they are simply narrative constructions that can only offer *interpretations* of the reality.

'Stories' are all around Marlow, whether in the form of a popular song, a piece of medical discourse, a psychoanalytical reading of his life, a religious sermon or his own detective story. They determine and contain his view of himself and the world around him. Like a 'prison sentence', it is language (and the stories it tells) that has partly kept him in chains. However, it seems that there is also something about language and storytelling that Marlow only slowly begins to understand. As he painfully rewrites his own work of fiction and reinterprets it, with the help of Dr Gibbon, so he finally starts to see its potential for self-revision. 'For the first time in my life,' Marlow tells the physiotherapist as he painfully grips his pen, 'I shall have to really think about the *value* of each and every little word. That's dangerous, that is' (225). Stories may imprison us, but if we use them with great care and attention they may also liberate us, giving us the potential to reinvent ourselves. As he rewrites his songs and stories in his head so Marlow gradually learns the act of 'rewriting' himself.

116

6 Salvation

And *though* after my skin *worms* destroy this *body*, yet in my flesh I shall
see God.

The Book of Job (emphasis in the original, 19: 26, KJV)

In Potter's last interview before his death from cancer in 1994 he
described *The Singing Detective* as simply the story of 'seeing a man
take up his bed and walk' (1994: 12).[35] The parable that the dramatist
refers to here comes from St Mark, which is also the name of the main
character in Marlow's detective novel. 'Mark,' says Amanda (Charon
Bourke) to Binney, '– it is Mark, isn't it – ?' 'As in the second gospel'
(23) is his reply. This particular parable concerns a paralysed man who
is taken to see Jesus. He is poor and rejected by the religious authorities
because his afflictions would have been attributed to sin. However, Jesus
does not judge him, he recognises his faith and immediately tells him
that 'You are at this moment forgiven' (Mark: 2.5). This statement was
seen as highly contentious because it was believed that only God could
forgive sin. It is here that Mark first introduces the notion of Jesus as
'Son of Man', saying that this 'God-man' has the power to forgive.

It could be argued that this parable directly goes against the
concept of original sin as outlined in Genesis, that is, the belief that Man
is essentially wicked because of Adam and Eve's original transgressions.
By forgiving this paralysed man Jesus is implying that sin is not
hereditary or unchangeable. When he tells the man to 'Arise, and take

up thy bed, and walk', he is implicitly urging the man to take his destiny into his own hands. It is only when he no longer considers himself a *victim* of fate that he can begin to take action. Ironically, it is his conception of himself as sinful and outside of society that ultimately denies him his humanity. Forgiveness unlocks the doors of his self-imprisonment and sets him free. According to theologian Simon Barrow, the 'Markan typology' looks something like this (Barrow, 2003):

Action	Effect	Outcome	(Cost)
Stand	humanity affirmed	a victim restored	(stripped)
Take	dignity claimed	a system challenged	(enslaved)
Walk	purpose declared	a destiny joined	(mortal)

When we first meet Marlow he is in a similar position to the paralysed man before he meets Jesus. The forest incident of his childhood has left him riddled with guilt to such a degree that it feels like an 'original sin'. He also clearly sees himself as a passive victim and one who exists outside of humanity; a sense of shame and indignity that denies him entry into society. He desperately seeks forgiveness for his 'sins' but does not realise that forgiveness lies within himself, that the sins of the past and his inability to overcome them are the very things that are making him ill. If Marlow is to become well again, then he must stop thinking of himself as inherently sinful – he must take ownership over his life and by doing so reconfirm his humanity.

As we have seen, Marlow begins his journey in a desperate state of denial. Rather than take responsibility for his own actions, he lashes out on what seems to him to be a faithless and corrupt world. When asked by the Registrar what he believes in, his reply reveals a deeply pessimistic, cynical and spiritually bankrupt man. 'I . . . believe in cholesterol,' he says, 'cigarettes, alcohol, masturbation, carbon monoxide, the Arts council, nuclear weapons, the *Daily Telegraph*, and not properly labelling fatal poisons' (40). But, as Duncan Wu explains, this is more than simple atheism; Potter's 'intoxicated expressions of disgust are significant because they expose not despair but the vacuum left by the absence of belief' (Wu, 1995: 36). In this 'absence of belief' Marlow rejects that there is anything other than random luck at work in the world (171):

> MARLOW: The rain, it falls. The sun, it shines. The wind blows. And that's what it's like. You're buffeted by this, by that, and it is nothing to do with you. Someone you love dies, or leaves. You get ill or you get better. You grow old and you remember, or you forget. And all the time everywhere, there is this canopy stretching over you.
> GIBBON: (*Determined to interrupt*) What canopy?
> *Marlow stops. Glares. Seems to speak, doesn't. Then does.*
> MARLOW: Things-as-they-are (*Almost laughs in scorn*) Fate. Fate. Impersonal. Irrational. Disinterested. The rain falls. The sun shines. The wind blows. . . . Fate (*Little shrug.*) Why not? S'good old word.

Such an extremely fatalistic view of life tends to suggest that there is actually little we can do to change ourselves or our fortunes. This has undertones of original sin in the sense that suffering is something we must simply accept because its roots are forever beyond our control. From this perspective, hereditary illness and hereditary sin have both put Marlow in his hospital bed and there is little in his own power to change it. 'God! Talk about the Book of Job,' he tells the doctors and nurses, '. . . I'm a prisoner in my . . . own skin . . . and bones' (28).

This reference to the Book of Job is not likely to be accidental. Job is a good man but Satan suggests to God that his goodness is based only on his comfortable existence. God therefore allows Satan to torment Job in order to test his piety and obedience, at one point even covering his entire body in painful and disfiguring boils. However, because he is a righteous man Job refuses to believe that his suffering is a result of past misdemeanours and therefore implicitly rejects the notion of original sin. This raises the possibility that God sometimes acts in capricious ways and Job's wife urges him to curse God and die. Instead, Job patiently responds with, 'Naked came I out of my mother's womb,

119

and naked shall I return thither; the Lord gave, and the Lord hath taken away; blessed be the name of the Lord' (Job: 1:21).

According to the *New Bible Commentary*, the story of Job teaches us 'equanimity'. 'I think the "trick" of a balanced, mature personality is equanimity. Equanimity. This is exactly what Job displayed. Equanimity in the face of disaster. What God displays is a "divine confidence" in Job' (Heavenor, 1970: 442). From the 'patience of Job' we learn what it means to maintain fidelity to God, even under great trials. This is perhaps why God does not intervene to help lessen Job's suffering at the hands of Satan. He knows that Job must learn this himself, that suffering forces him to contemplate the notion of sin and his relationship with God. 'How long can you go on seeing things through a blinding rage,' the Registrar asks Marlow, '. . . where are you going to find some equanimity?' (Potter, 1996: 40).

Like Job, Marlow must learn that human suffering is not necessarily a punishment from God, that even good men will suffer and

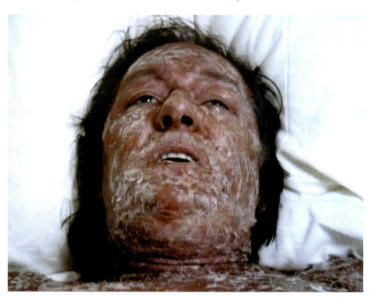

'Talk about the book of Job'

that suffering must be endured with patience and self-control. It is when he stops blaming outside forces (such as fate or past sins) for his condition that he begins to take responsibility for the state of his own health. Marlow can go on forever blaming the past for his condition or he can decide to take his destiny in his own hands and transform his life. Although the childhood incidents may have felt like an 'original sin' from which he could never escape, he gradually learns that the past does not have to imprison him for ever. This is made clear in the first episode when he asks the Registrar whether he will ever be free of his illness. 'You ask those questions', he tells him, 'as though someone else was responsible for your condition. But no one is, or, at least, in the unlikely event that someone, anyone, is – then that someone cannot be anyone other than yourself' (39).

In contrast to original sin, the notion of forgiveness implies that action *can* be taken to change the world around us, that we are not all doomed to suffer for the mistakes of past generations and that we can change our fates and the fates of those around us. Marlow has to forgive himself if he wants to recover and realise that none of the things that took place during his childhood were actually his fault. As he does this, so his conception of himself transforms from a *passive* victim to someone who takes an *active* role in determining his own destiny. In this way, Marlow moves from an essentially voyeuristic view of the world to one that deals directly with life. Like Jeff (James Stewart) in Hitchcock's *Rear Window* (1954), Marlow must stop experiencing life from a safe distance and learn to interact directly with the people and the world around him, particularly the woman he loves. '[I]sn't it about time you climbed out of your tree?' (243) Nicola asks him in the final episode.

As Marlow begins to understand all of this so his illness gradually lessens and he is eventually able to heal himself. He has unconsciously used his skin condition to be apart from society and to keep others at a distance, perhaps mirroring Cain's own self-imposed exile East of Eden. Instead of blaming others, he must now take responsibility for his illness and in doing so take responsibility for his

121

recovery also. What this suggests is that the hell into which Marlow has descended is actually of his own making. It is not God punishing him (as the Old Testament rants of the schoolmistress might imply) but himself. No wonder, then, that we find Marlow reciting from his other namesake Christopher Marlowe's *The Tragical History of Doctor Faustus* (1604), a play about a man who makes a pact with the devil. Not believing in eternal life, Faust sells his soul for power and knowledge. However, as his life spirals into decay he soon realises that hell is not a geographical place or location but is a subjective and psychological state of mind (only in the published script) (22): 'Hell hath no limits nor is circumscrib'd / In one self place, where we are is Hell, / And where Hell is, there must we ever be –'.

This movement from 'passive observer' (hell is a geographical location) to 'active interpreter' (we make our own hell) is mirrored in Marlow's complex relationship with his own detective story. At first he appears to accept it as a straightforward crime story, one which now simply offers him a form of distraction from his terrible predicament. However, with the help of Gibbon he begins to see that it is a great deal more than that. Rather than accepting it at face value (i.e. its meaning is transparent and unchangeable) he begins to 'interact' with the text and he starts to discover different meanings within it. In other words, Marlow gradually realises that the meaning of his story is not fixed; that reader interpretation will inevitably offer different meanings and that the text itself is always open to change and reinvention. As he does this, so he begins to understand that the meaning of any story is always open to various interpretations.

The origin of this realisation comes when Marlow begins to acknowledge and appreciate just how much of his own emotional psychology is in his formulaic pulp novel. Mark Binney's encounter with Sonia is almost identical to Marlow's real encounter with a prostitute.[36] Not only are their apartments the same but much of the dialogue is repeated. This is further emphasised by the same actress (Kate McKenzie) playing the different roles. Mark Binney's name in the novel is also explicitly connected with Mrs Marlow's lover (Raymond

Binney), Nicola's imaginary lover (Mark Finney) and the classroom scapegoat (Mark Binney), suggesting that the characters represent some deeply buried anxieties in his own life. Gibbon is also shocked to be told that Mrs Marlow killed herself by drowning – exactly the same fate that awaits Sonia in his story. Marlow may have authored 'The Singing Detective' but he seems strangely unaware of how much of himself is actually in it.[37]

  Marlow's inability to appreciate the psychological subtext of his own detective story subtly suggests that meaning does not ultimately reside at the site of the author. Rather than an author 'anchoring' the meaning of a story in a rigid or fixed manner, an understanding of a text is always open.[38] As such, the meaning of his story does not belong to its author, it belongs to everyone who reads it; stories (just like his childhood songs) are always open to reinterpretation. As Roland Barthes famously put it in 'The Death of the Author' (1977: 148):

129

Fact

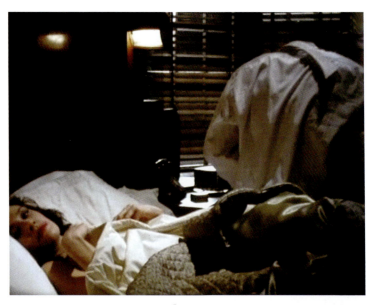

Fiction

a text is made up of multiple meanings, drawn from many cultures and
entering into mutual relations of dialogue, parody, contestation, but there is
one place where this multiplicity is focused and that place is the reader,
not, as was hitherto said, the author. The reader is the space on which all
the quotations that make up a writing are inscribed without any of them
being lost; a text's unity lies not in its origin but in its destination.

Many of these themes appear to come to a head when Reginald
discovers that the author of the book he is reading ('The Singing
Detective' no less) is actually in the same hospital ward as he is. Adding
yet another level of self-reflexivity to the serial as a whole, Reginald goes
to him in the hope of enlightenment. 'Who killed her?' he asks, '[W]ho
put her in the river?' 'Oh, you'll find out,' Marlow replies, '[b]ut only by
reading it' (188). This implicit emphasis on 'the role of the reader' does
suggest a refusal to accept an authorial truth, allowing meaning to be

generated by the reader rather than having it prescribed and determined by something or someone outside the text.

When the fictional detective shoots the real Marlow in the head in the final episode, we perhaps witness first-hand the 'death of the author'. The fictional detective is finally granted a life of his own because meaning is no longer fixed at one place. But, of course, this is also a liberation for Marlow, for the author is no longer tied to only one story and one interpretation. As Barthes explains, the death of the author will gradually bring about 'the birth of the reader' (1977: 148). After Marlow's symbolic death he certainly appears 'reborn', perhaps suggesting that even 'life stories' are open to revision and rewriting. Rather than simply accepting the 'story' that has been given to him, he begins to reinterpret it and in doing so rewrite himself. [39]

Appropriately enough, Reginald has almost the last word of the serial as he 'laboriously' comes to the end of Marlow's novel. 'And-her-soft-red-lips-clam-*clamped*-themselves-on his. The-End (*he lowers*

The death of the author

the book). Lucky devil!' (248–9). In Reginald's eyes the hero of
Marlow's book is a 'lucky devil', not quite the way that its author would
probably see it. However, considering his miraculous recovery the
reader may have a better understanding of the detective novel's
optimistic ending than its own author. Like its hero, Marlow does
finally 'get the girl' as Nicola arrives to take him home.

Inevitably linked to these debates around meaning and
authorship is the ultimate 'Author' – God. Transferring these questions
to a spiritual level it forces us to ask who the 'author' of our own lives
really is. Are we simply at the mercy of God's authorial power or can we
take our lives in our own hands and rewrite the script we have been
given? This may also help explain why there are so many incidents in the
serial of watching and being watched – the voyeuristic universe that
Marlow lives in also appears to be presided over by an essentially
omnipotent God. Although we may feel that we can determine our own
fate, there are often hints and suggestions in Potter's work that our lives

The birth of the reader

are being 'written' for us. These are questions that the serial returns to time and time again; it offers a meditation on the notion of personal sovereignty and authorship that asks some of the biggest questions of all – who or what controls the shape of our lives and where does the real power and potential for change and renewal lie?

Such an understanding of authorship implicitly allows the power of the *reader* to change and 'rewrite' the stories they are given. While realism arguably seems to allow little room for reader interpretation, there are those stories that seem to exploit and even celebrate textual indeterminacy. These types of narratives are what Umberto Eco refers to as 'open' texts, those which encourage readers to actively participate in the production of meaning (see Eco, 1979). *The Singing Detective* appears to embody many of the characteristics of the 'open' text, its self-reflexive narrative confusion seemingly celebrating textual ambiguity and uncertainty. According to Catrin Prys, '[a]lthough *The Singing Detective* does search and (to an extent) reveals a central thread or a core of meaning, it would be misleading to suggest that the narrative itself is not "open" to a whole array of narrative spaces and textual indeterminacies' (Prys, forthcoming).

The Singing Detective's 'open' and self-reflexive narrative has led many critics to conclude that it is a work of postmodern fiction (see, for example, Corrigan, 1991; Bondebjerg, 1992; Gras, 2000). Postmodernism shares post-structuralism's notion of the real as having been constructed and mediated by language and this leads to a distrust of 'meta-narratives'. Meta-narratives are those grand theories such as Marxism, Christianity and Freudian psychoanalysis that aim to tell us the truth about the world but are actually only linguistic accounts (narratives or stories) of reality. This means that postmodern literature tends to implicitly deconstruct any notion of an absolute 'truth'. It therefore tends to be playful, ironic and self-referential to the point where meaning is consistently undermined and the process of storytelling itself is exposed. As Peter Brooker explains, it results in 'a self-ironic eclecticism and knowingness, experienced by media-wise audiences and readers along with the postmodern artist, all well versed in the use of key postmodern devices of pastiche, parody, recycling and sampling' (1999: 203).

The two nameless 'Mysterious Men' certainly seem like a master-class in postmodern meta-fiction, their artificial construction being foregrounded to the point of comic absurdity. 'We're padding,' says one of them. 'Like a couple of bleed'n sofas' (231). They perhaps most resemble Tom Stoppard's Rosencrantz and Guildenstern in *Rosencrantz and Guildenstern Are Dead* (1967), later made into a film of the same name (Stoppard, 1990).[40] Added to this, the serial's absorption of and delight in popular culture (pop music, detective fiction, situation comedy and so on) seems to reflect the postmodern breakdown in the stability of artistic and cultural hierarchies. Similarly, the serial's pronounced use of genre and its flamboyant subversion of narrative conventions appear to deliberately draw the viewer's attention to the drama's artificial form.

128

Two mysterious men

However, unlike *Twin Peaks* (ABC, 1991) where the revelation of who murdered Laura Palmer is almost continually deferred, in *The Singing Detective* we do finally find out 'whodunnit'.[41] From pulp fiction, popular music, parody and the serial's endless ruminations over storytelling, Marlow does gradually 'crack the case'. Indeed, I would argue that the serial is defined by its ability to harness the apparently 'empty' and 'depthless' signs of postmodern culture and breathe true meaning and significance back into them. Rather than simply celebrating a postmodern world, it investigates and critiques it until meaning is gradually revealed and vestiges of depth and significance are finally discovered in its pulp culture and its dizzy array of shiny surfaces (see Nelson, 1987: 200–7). While its multilayered narrative may well offer a complex and self-reflexive 'hall of mirrors', in the end all the reflections lead back to one authentic self. Given only the consumerist products of commercial art with which to rebuild himself, our hero nonetheless transforms them into something resembling a true expression of personal identity. It is for this reason that the serial is often referred to as an example of classic modernism and perhaps even an implicit critique of a depthless 'postmodern' culture (see Creeber, 1996; Cook, 1998; Caughie, 2000).

129

Indeed, *The Singing Detective* seems to reject the postmodern and post-structuralist notion that reality and subjectivity are *entirely* constructed by language. 'In the long, grey, ebb tide of so-named Post-Modernism,' Potter wrote in 1987, 'pseudo-totalitarian, illiberal, and dehumanizing theories and practices lie on top of the cold waters like a huge and especially filthy oil slick. The birds can no longer beat their wings' (Potter, 1987: 26). For Potter, then, postmodern theory inevitably dehumanises us, even threatening to 'pollute' the natural world. In contrast, he consistently argued that there is a *real* and *authentic* individual within us all that is beyond discourse and society. This individual 'spirit' he most often referred to in interviews and writings as 'the sovereign self'. For Potter, the 'sovereign self' was the 'most precious of all human capacities' and existed 'even beyond language . . .' (1994: 71).

Such notions of the self tend to make Potter's work fundamentally humanist; consistently affirming that there is a something within each and every one of us that makes us more than just a piece of biological machinery. Consequently, his characters have to somehow move beyond the limits of everyday reality to find the very *core* of their being. This means understanding the self through an intense process of self-reflection. In particular, it involves making peace with one's past, but also accepting and appreciating the implicit and subtle connections that inevitably link our past and present selves together. As Chris Lippard explains (2000: 110):

> To realize the sense of a coherent subjectivity – a sovereign self – Dennis Potter's characters must free themselves from personal fixations and societal constraints – a theme that remains significant in all his drama. To seek to understand one's identity is the task that one must undertake in order to function satisfactorily; to achieve this self-awareness his characters must not only 'come to terms' with their pasts, but must be aware that past and present lie, intertwined, alongside each other.

This search for the self is essentially a spiritual quest for Potter's characters. Beyond language and the materiality of society lies a realm where his characters can connect with their 'sovereign selves' and in doing so commune with God. 'I would have liked to have used my pen to praise a loving God and all his loving creation,' Marlow tells a somewhat surprised Gibbon. 'I would have liked to have seen hosts of radiant and translucent angels climbing along spinning shafts of golden light deeper and deeper into the blue caverns of heaven' (57). Such poetic and religious discourse suggests that Marlow's faith is never altogether lost, that his sense of a sovereign self (beyond language and the material world) offers him a glimpse into a more spiritual realm.

Seen in this light, *The Singing Detective*'s conception of the self is perhaps more linked to elements of Romanticism than modernism or postmodernism. Romanticism can partly be seen as a reaction against the rationalisation of nature by the Enlightenment. William Blake's illustration of Sir Isaac Newton reducing the world to a mathematical formula with his compass and map is perhaps the most famous illustration of this philosophy; science and reason tending to diminish the power of creativity and imagination. In contrast, Romanticism believed in the possibility of the human spirit to break free of the confines of rationalism, and experience 'sublimity' through a connection with nature. As in William Wordsworth's poem 'Tintern Abbey', the Romantics longed to experience that moment when 'We see into the life of things', when we feel '. . . a sense sublime/Of something far more deeply interfused' (1974: 206–7).[42]

For the Romantics, the power of the 'holy imagination' is most often glimpsed in childhood, a vision of the world that we inevitably lose in maturity. According to Wordsworth's 'Ode: Intimations of Immortality from Recollections of Early Childhood', 'Heaven lies about us in our infancy', but soon 'Shades of the prison-house begin to close' (ibid.: 587). The philosophical implication of this notion of childhood is perhaps also best summed up by Wordsworth in his now famous statement that 'the child is father of the man' (ibid.: 79). By this, he seems to imply that children possess a superior perception of nature than adults and so are 'wiser' and more at peace with the world around them. It also suggests that the child 'gives birth' to the man in the sense that the adult is formed by childhood experience. Consequently, Romanticism vehemently rejected the notion of original sin, arguing that all children are inherently innocent and are corrupted by the confines of society and social conformity. 'Let us lay down as an incontrovertible rule', wrote Jean Jacques Rousseau, 'that the first impulses of nature are always right; there is no original sin in the human heart; the how and why of the entrance of every vice can be traced' (cited by Coveney, 1957: 8).[43]

Connected with this notion of the self is the Romantic challenge to the Christian split between the 'spirit' and the 'flesh'. The body and the soul are almost separate entities for traditional Christianity, the flesh associated with the 'animal' and the spirit with the 'divine'. Consequently, we can only find God by overcoming the 'animal' in us and striving for a more 'heavenly' realm. This, of course, has sexual

131

implications as the 'flesh' and the 'animal' are explicitly joined in the act of human copulation. In contrast, the Romantics consistently contested such a rigid divide, arguing that both the body and the soul are part of the 'holy imagination'. For William Blake, sex is simply a part of life and no one can be superior to it or be honestly content with less than true gratification. Blake's reading of the Book of Job particularly refuses to accept the 'flesh' and 'spirit' divide. Job eventually learns that the body is not just the 'shell' in which his soul is kept but also an essential part of his spirit. This is something that he only comes to understand through intense physical suffering that, ironically, brings him closer to God (see Cook, 1998: 138–40). As Northrop Frye puts it (1969: 194):

> The transformation of the body into a spiritual substance is the Christian doctrine of bodily resurrection. Job puts this doctrine in the form of its essential paradox: 'And though after my skin worms destroy this body, yet in my flesh I shall see God'. There is no soul imprisoned within the body evaporating at death, but a living man armed with all the powers of his present body, infinitely expanded. The relation of soul to body is that of an oak to an acorn, not of a genie to a bottle.

As this suggests, there is clearly a discernibly Romantic impulse in *The Singing Detective*; the adult Marlow longs to reclaim the natural and innocent sense of the world that he once glimpsed as a child. This was before he was taught to divide it into the 'dirty' and the 'clean', the 'spirit' and the 'flesh' or even to see women simply as 'angels' and 'whores'. Fighting against the rationalism of various institutional discourses, he must rediscover and nourish that core of himself that lies beyond language and see the world as it truly is. Through his physical suffering Marlow begins to realise that his painful body is ironically the very source through which he is able to reclaim his 'sovereign self' and commune again with God. Like Job, he desperately searches for reasons to explain his suffering, but the only real answer he finds is that pain catalyses individual development in such a way that a life without it cannot develop. Despite Marlow's desperate plight, he does finally find a

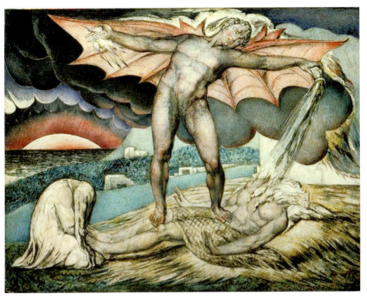

William Blake, *Satan Smiting Job with Sore Boils*, c. 1826 (Tate Gallery)   133

renewed faith in the world, his slow return to society clearly discernible in the improvement of his skin condition over the six episodes. By the end of the serial Marlow *is* able to walk out of the hospital and return to society, seemingly reborn.

'I wandered lonely as a cloud ...', Mr Hall recites out loud. 'Poetry. That's more my taste. I don't want corpses all over the place' (225). In his cultural snobbery Mr Hall may think that Wordsworth's poetry is more valuable than detective fiction but, ironically, they are both about the investigation of the self and the re-examination of past events. It is the mulling over of the 'corpses' of his past that will gradually make Marlow well, helping him to find a place of equanimity where child and man are eventually reunited. In this sense, Philip's fall from grace is inevitable (it is simply part of maturing), but by regaining that childish sense of wonder that loss or Fall can be reversed. As Potter put it (Fuller, 1993: 46):

> Our first allegiances are based on Eden. The whole story of human culture
> is based upon original sin. It's an inescapable fact of our mortality. When
> we're young we feel the 'the bright shoots of everlastingness' but later we
> laugh at that, and we laugh tenderly. We laugh with a mixture of awe and
> regret, because we know it cannot be sustained. But if we lose it altogether
> then we lose something essential, we lose the bud in the flower, we lose the
> possibilities of regeneration.

The continual need for personal regeneration is perhaps implicitly
suggested at the end of the serial. Marlow's slow walk out of the
hospital with his wife is accompanied by the classic wartime song 'We'll
Meet Again', sung by Vera Lynn. Who or what exactly he will 'meet
again' is not clear. Of course, it could be an allusion to his successful
reunion with Nicola. However, it could also suggest that the problems
in Marlow's life are not entirely over, that the 'ghosts' of his past and his
illness will never quite leave him. Whatever the precise significance of
the song, it does subtly suggest that self-revision is a continuing process.
Unlike stories, which have neat and tidy endings, real life continues
without ever being completely summed up or explained. Marlow may
now understand himself better through the power of personal detective
work, but unlike the conclusion of a typical detective novel there are still
'loose ends' in his life that will perhaps never be completely worked out
or fully understood.

134

The Singing Detective is essentially about stories; the way
stories hurt and imprison us (as in the Old Testament's pessimistic
notion of original sin), the way stories can inform us about ourselves (as
in the psychological subtext revealed in Marlow's detective story) and
ultimately about how stories can heal us (as in Marlow's act of revising
his own work and eventually his own life). It is difficult to disentangle all
these thematic threads into one coherent and linear trajectory. However,
I hope this overall interrogation into the nature of storytelling helps to
bring a collection of discourses together (biblical, psychoanalytical,
medical, sexual, musical, fictional and so on) in such a way that it
touches upon a number of important issues within the serial as a whole.

'We'll Meet Again'

Seen in this light, the central story of *The Singing Detective* is the way that one man learns to disregard the 'story' given to him and replace it with a new 'story' – one that allows him to control his life and eventually become the 'author' of his own fate.

As I indicated in the Introduction, *The Singing Detective* is so complex and ambiguous at times that to reduce it to a single meaning would be simplistic and would not do justice to its thematic and stylistic intricacy. Thus, although I may have uncovered a few 'clues' I do not pretend to have found any real 'solutions'; except perhaps for this – that there is always potential for human change and renewal and that the stories of our lives are forever open to retelling and revision. Stories may often imprison us but they can sometimes be the very means by which we can also set ourselves free. This optimistic outlook on the transformative power of the human spirit may well be the final legacy of *The Singing Detective*. 'Minute by minute, we make this world,' Marlow reminds us. 'We make our own world' (96).

Conclusion

Marlow: (*Sigh*) That's all folks.

Dennis Potter, *The Singing Detective* (1986): 85

Despite some favourable reviews, most critics were not kind to the big screen version of *The Singing Detective*. 'A lot has been lost in translation,' wrote A. O. Scott in *The New York Times* (Scott, 2006):

> On its way to the big screen, Potter's intricate, fascinating story has shrunk. The ideas that lurked in the mini-series' shadows and alleyways are now placed squarely in the spotlight, where they look obvious and thin . . . The movie lurches when it should glide, shouts when it should whisper and mumbles when it should sing.

'The musical numbers are staged with no flair,' wrote Matthew De Abaitua (De Abaitua, 2006):

> the miming shoddily synched and performed with tangible embarrassment (that means you Saul Rubinek). The scatology, political incorrectness and sex scenes that made the TV series so notorious are no big deal on the big screen, and Downey Jr never says anything *that* inappropriate.

This is not a place for a full and detailed discussion of the film, but the reason for its lack of success may well tell us something about why the original television serial worked so well. Ironically, part of the problem with the film version seemed to be the script, which Potter rewrote himself. The writer relocated the action from Britain to America, an economic and cultural necessity for Hollywood that did not alter the actual story significantly. However, to set it in a contemporary world he made his central protagonist grow up in the 1950s rather than the 1940s, even changing the name of Philip Marlow to Dan Dark (perhaps to reflect that particular era of pulp fiction).[44] This small alteration in time did change things greatly. For example, the songs were now from a later decade (the 1950s). The doctors and nurses are now seen dancing to Danny & The Juniors' 'At the Hop', a bouncy rock'n'roll song with seemingly little lyrical significance to the story and with none of the strange, sinister and religious undertones of 'Dry Bones'.[45] Similarly, while the film noir sequences were confidently directed by Keith Gordon, they seemed to lack the dark, eerie and foreboding feel of Amiel's generic pastiche. Perhaps its director preferred to heighten the story's shiny 'postmodern' surfaces, but it did little to capture the real heart and soul of this tragic and desperate story.

137

Perhaps the main problem with Potter's screenplay is that he had to edit so much of the original in order to make it fit the smaller requirements of cinema. This meant cutting over seven hours of material into just one hour and forty-nine minutes. This was no easy task, considering the multilayered complexity of the original episodic drama with all its subplots, generic hybridity and narrative twists and turns. Serial television gives a writer a huge canvas on which to work while also giving the viewer (particularly if it is watched in weekly episodes) a sense of the passing of time that cinema can never quite match. The temporal breadth of the original serial is one of its greatest strengths; the long therapeutic process covers six separate episodes, a process that allows an audience to fully appreciate and believe in Marlow's painfully slow recovery (see Creeber, 2004).

Cutting so much of the script also meant that a great deal of the original story was lost; many of the more subtle elements of the drama were simply taken out or briefly sketched over. Putting Dark in a private room on his own, for example, meant that there was no need to have him or the medical staff interact with other patients, thereby eradicating so much of the humour and colour of the original script. All the schoolroom scenes were also cut out; while these flashbacks to his childhood were not essential to the plot they potentially added so much depth to Marlow's troubled psychological make-up. It was for television that Potter primarily wrote and the serial nature of the medium meant that it was often difficult to adapt such large and complex narratives to a single film.

Although Robert Downey Jr puts in a strong performance as Dan Dark, it never really captures the jaded, cynical and vulnerable pessimism of Gambon's Philip Marlow. There was also perhaps a little too much of the film noir detective in Dark's hospital persona; his hard-boiled delivery seemingly present when he is simply meant to be talking naturally. While Downey clearly had to make the part his own, it is hard not to get the feeling that he was trying to reinvent a role which actually needed little reinvention. Against type, Mel Gibson (also producer) puts in a good performance as Dr Gibbon but it is perhaps not enough to save the film from slowly descending into an MTV pastiche of its former self. Even the make-up seemed unconvincing; Marlow's flaky and peeling skin is now replaced with large red blotches and sores. Perhaps it was an attempt to make his condition more realistic than the 'toned down' television version, but it somehow failed to reflect the fragility and seedy psoriatic despair which Francis Hannon's make-up gave to the part.

However, perhaps the biggest problem of all was the lack of money seemingly invested in the production as a whole. As Meagan Spencer put it (2006):

> maybe all this film needed was a bigger budget so that some flash could be lavished upon its ambitious subject matter. So the noir could be proper noir, the musical numbers could be proper Hollywood musical numbers, so that it could be convincing and reach the dizzying heights it promised with its multi-layered script. Instead, *The Singing Detective* came off looking as low rent as some of the back alleys the story was set in.

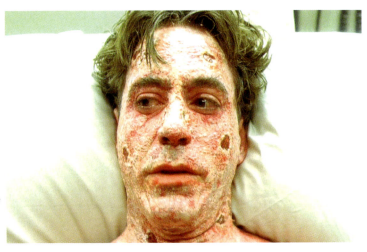

Dan Dark

There was something almost inevitable about the film's lack of critical success. The original television serial was such an extraordinary triumph of writing, directing, acting and production skills that any comparison was almost bound to disappoint. It was arguably the summit of Potter's career and possibly his lasting legacy. The work he did afterwards never quite matched its quality, originality and its sheer narrative ambition (even when he was rewriting his own masterpiece). Perhaps he became over-indulged by an industry that allowed him (despite his complete lack of experience) to even direct his own scripts.[46] The writer may have also increasingly surrounded himself with people who were less likely to criticise his ideas or push his creative abilities in the way that collaborators like Amiel and Trodd had done in the past. However, I believe it was primarily because the writer emptied so much of himself into *The Singing Detective* that there was little left for him to tap into creatively once it was completed. The serial seemed to exhaust Potter and he consequently tried to re-employ similar techniques (lip-synching, for example, was reused in *Lipstick on Your Collar*) but with little of the same success. The writer even acknowledged as much when, in the

139

posthumous *Karaoke*, its dying writer sadly remembers a time when he 'could make a whole ward *sing*' (emphasis in the original, Potter, 1996: 81).

The television version of *The Singing Detective* ends with a montage of earlier scenes from the story. This was something that Amiel and Potter apparently decided upon in the editing process and includes the nine-year-old Philip high in his beloved tree, smiling broadly for the first time. This smile seems to capture Marlow's renewed faith in himself and God, but it also appears to sum up neatly the joyous success of the serial as it reached its climatic conclusion – all the narrative and thematic threads finally coming together. *The Singing Detective* can quite rightly claim to be the *Citizen Kane* of the small screen; its extraordinary complexity, technical sophistication and artistic originality elevate it to the very best of its kind. It is a serial that helped to transform the medium and set the standards by which all television is now judged. Despite what Vera Lynn may sing at its conclusion, it is unlikely that we will ever meet its like again.

Notes

1 *The Singing Detective* was beaten by *Edge of Darkness* (BBC, 1985), *I, Claudius* (BBC, 1976), *Brideshead Revisited* (ITV, 1981) and *Boys from the Blackstuff* (BBC, 1982), which came out on top.

2 In *Stand Up, Nigel Barton*, Nigel (Keith Barron) steals the class daffodil and blames it on another boy. There is also a surprisingly similar scenario alluded to in Potter's first (semi-autobiographical) book, written while still at Oxford (Potter, 1960).

3 This is particularly true of Potter's original script of *Moonlight on the Highway*, before much of it was cut by the television authorities at the time (for an insightful discussion of the original script see Carpenter, 1998: 225–36).

4 Jack Black was also the name of an earlier Potter protagonist played by Denholm Elliot in *Follow the Yellow Brick Road* (BBC, 1972). This is typical of the playful intertextuality that Potter's drama so often deployed.

5 How important Amiel was in shaping the final serial is perhaps apparent when one considers the sharp decline in the success of Potter's drama immediately after *The Singing Detective*, particularly *Blackeyes* (BBC, 1989), which the writer (perhaps naively, considering his ill health and lack of experience) directed himself.

6 Trodd produced seventeen separate Potter productions in total, including the writer's last two posthumous serials, *Karaoke* (BBC/C4, 1996) and *Cold Lazarus* (C4/BBC, 1996).

7 According to Trodd, '[p]roducing Potter in the seventies and eighties involved the crucial mutation of script into film or play – all the creative, logistical and financial

interplay – but there were two other areas of struggle that did not apply to the other developing writers I took on. With Dennis, the fight for health and survival shadowed every project' (Trodd, 2000: 231–2).

8 It was a great surprise that Potter never received a BAFTA for *The Singing Detective*. According to Amiel, the awards that year were a 'sick joke'. 'That Dennis could be sitting there getting progressively drunker and not hear his name mentioned once was simply a crime. It got thirteen nominations from the membership but just two awards' (cited by Gilbert, 1995: 272). Perhaps this is one of the reasons why the Academy decided to name a writer's award in his name after his death in 1994.

9 This was an idea later utilised in Lars von Trier's miniseries *Riget* (*The Kingdom*) (Danish Television, 1994) and Stephen King's *Kingdom Hospital*.

10 The dialogue here was changed slightly from the original script in order to make the humour more obvious. This quote reflects these small changes.

11 *Music From The Singing Detective* (soundtrack) (Wmo), *Music From The Singing Detective and More* (Golden Stars) and *Songs From The Singing Detective and More* (Platinum).

12 This 'seamlessness' is unlike Eisenstein's conception of editing as 'dynamic and discontinuous'. However, there is clearly an attempt to produce a 'heightened' or 'expressionistic' reality, which is pushing the limits of traditional realism.

13 Proust is perhaps best known as the author of *À la recherche du temps perdu*

(*Remembrance of Things Past* [1913–27]). Arguably, the key scene in the novel is when a madeleine cake (a small, rich cookie-like pastry) enables the narrator to experience the past completely as a simultaneous part of his present existence. To explore the connection between Freud and Proust see Bowie (1987).

14 Williamson was also in *The Cheap Detective* (Moore, 1987), a spoof comedy movie written by Neil Simon, which starred Peter Falk as Lou Peckinpaugh, a detective also in the Humphrey Bogart mould and an affectionate parody of movies such as *Casablanca* (Curtiz, 1942) and *The Maltese Falcon* (Huston, 1931).

15 This Oedipal dimension is made even more explicit in *The Seven-Per-Cent Solution* by having the man who sleeps with Holmes' mother to be Professor Moriarty, the detective's arch rival.

16 'Skinscapes' in Potter's published script.

17 In recent times one thinks of Aids, some commentators suggesting that there was a direct connection between the disease and the 'sins' of homosexuality.

18 Potter has insisted in interview that he never explicitly refers to the Forest of Dean anywhere in the script of *The Singing Detective* (Potter, 1994: 70). However, most of those familiar with his work would recognise the landscape and working-class culture as being directly from Potter's childhood home, even if it was not explicitly spelled out by Potter himself.

19 'Thee' and 'thou' are still used today in Welsh, in the form of 'ti' and 'chi'.

20 This direct address to camera is reminiscent of its use in *Stand Up, Nigel Barton*, when we are encouraged to see particular scenes as a memory (filtered through Marlow's mind), rather than a complete and actual movement back in time.

21 Amiel's theory is that 'it was all to do with the Beeb-bashing period that Thatcher and Murdoch joined forces on so that he could advance his interest in Sky. It was whipped up by the Murdoch press' (cited by Gilbert, 1995: 271).

22 Whitehouse suggested on Radio 4 that Potter's real mother had actually committed adultery like Marlow's mother. Potter's mother was understandably upset and successfully sued *The Listener* (which later published the article) for libel and won (see Creeber, 1998a: 11).

23 Of course, there are other reasons for Mrs Marlow's suicide; she is trapped in a lifeless marriage and living unhappily with her in-laws many miles away from home. However, this is clearly the event that finally sparks the tragedy. Hammersmith Bridge is a recurring location in Potter's work (see, for example, the ending of *Pennies from Heaven* when Arthur is miraculously reunited with Eileen). Potter himself lived nearby the bridge as a child when he stayed with his mother's relatives in London.

24 Mr Marlow's cry here is very reminiscent of the horrific scream let out by Donald Sutherland in Roeg's *Don't Look Now* on discovering the body of his drowned daughter.

25 Potter's script actually has Mrs Marlow just say 'Oh stay! Stay!' The dialogue in the actual drama makes it more explicit.

26 'Oh those moments after we made love,' remembers Daniel Miller in *Hide and Seek*, '[t]he gloom that fell upon me was deep enough to make me want to die' (1973: 156).

27 This passage is strikingly similar to a passage in Potter's own novel, *Hide and Seek*: 'I am disgusted by the thought of spoiled human flesh. Mouth upon mouth, tongue against tongue, limb upon limb, skin rubbing at skin. Faces contort and organs spurt out a smelly stain, a sticky betrayal. The crudest joke against the human race lies in that sweaty farce by which we are first formed and given life. No wonder we carry about us a sense of inescapable loss, a burden of original sin, and a propensity to wild, anguished violence' (1973: 118–19). What this seems to imply is that Potter was possibly examining the misogyny is his own work.

28 Much fuss has been made about the revelations in Humphrey Carpenter's biography that Potter actually visited prostitutes (see Carpenter, 1998: 135–8). Whatever the truth is about this, Potter clearly saw prostitutes as representing something significant in his dramatic landscape and this is all that is relevant to this particular critique.

29 The protagonist of *Moonlight on the Highway* (David Peters, who shares the same initials as the writer) is sexually abused as a child and develops a profound neurosis as a result. According to Carpenter, he has 'two personalities where love and sex are concerned: the compulsive user of prostitutes, and the idolizer of unreal sexless dream girls' (Carpenter, 1998: 235). Incidentally, he also has a strange and intense relationship with his mother.

30 These ideas were pursued and developed by Potter in *Blackeyes*; his attempt to write a feminist drama that critiqued the exploitation and objectification of women by men. The fact that the serial was heavily criticised for ironically exploiting and manipulating its central female character (Gina Bellman) suggests that Potter may not have exorcised the misogyny implicit in his past work as much as he had hoped (see Creeber, 1998a: 178–86).

31 Ingrid Bergman's character actually says 'Play it, Sam. Play "As Time Goes By".' Only later Bogart says, 'You played it for her, you can play it for me!'

32 In this respect *The Singing Detective* pre-empts *The Sopranos* (HBO, 1999 –) with its psychiatric deconstruction of the archetypal male figure (in this case, the mobster). Indeed, in one scene in the first series there seems to be a nod towards *The Singing Detective* when the young Tony Soprano hides behind a tree as he watches his father carry out a vicious act of violence (his innocence dramatically shattered as he realises what his father actually does for a living). Notice also Tony Soprano's difficult relationship with his mother. She even threatens to blind him in the same flashback, clearly suggesting Oedipal connections.

33 Richard Hoggart was a leading figure in British cultural studies during the 1950s, 1960s and 1970s. In particular, his book *The Uses of Literacy* (1957) shares a great deal in common with many Potter themes – including a preoccupation with social class, 1930s popular music and pulp literature (see Creeber, 2000; Voigts-Virchow, 2000).

143

34 Potter's *Where Adam Stood* (BBC, 1976) was inspired by the autobiography of Edmund Gosse and portrayed a father's attempt to reconcile the scientific discoveries of Charles Darwin and his own literal belief in the Old Testament. Gibbon's name could also, of course, just refer to the suggestion that all doctors are monkeys. This reading would not be out of place with Potter's often dark and absurd humour.

35 Early in 1994 Potter was diagnosed with terminal cancer. With only a few months to live he was invited by Michael Grade to appear on Channels 4's *Without Walls*, interviewed by Melvyn Bragg. The interview is now available in script form (see Potter, 1994) and as a video entitled *Seeing the Blossom: An Interview with Dennis Potter* (C4, 1994).

36 Notice the poster on Marlow's wall in this scene is that of *Blow Up* (Antonioni, 1966), a film with a similar obsession with the primal scene. Its male protagonist witnesses a couple making love in a park, explicitly placing him within a voyeuristic position (as he – unknown to them – photographs them).

37 Marlow's apparent lack of insight about the personal implications of his own novel was bizarrely mirrored by Potter's own relationship with *The Singing Detective*. Amiel recalls that at the end of a read-through (with Potter reading the part of the Schoolmistress) he went 'white in the face'. 'I never realized this thing', he told him, 'was so fucking close to the bone' (cited by Carpenter, 1998: 453).

38 This may help explain why Potter was so adamant that *The Singing Detective* was not simply biographical and that he was actually playing with the '*form* of autobiography' (cited by Fuller, 1993: 95). Like detective fiction and psychoanalysis, autobiography is simply another 'genre' that has its own set of narrative rules and linguistic conventions. This means that biography is never an exact view of the past for it is always manipulated, distorted and highly subjective in its representation of historical events.

39 A similar ending comes at the conclusion of Allen's *Play it Again, Sam*. 'Well, I guess you won't be needing me any more,' Bogart tells Allen. 'There's nothing I can tell you now that you don't already know.' 'I guess that's so,' he replies. 'I guess the secret's not being you, it's being me.'

40 The film version starred Gary Oldman, who also took the lead in Potter and Roeg's *Track 29*.

41 In *Twin Peaks* we do ultimately find out that Laura was killed by her father, but while he was under the influence of the spirit 'Bob'. Many viewers seemed to find this an unsatisfactory conclusion and viewing figures apparently declined after this ambiguous revelation.

42 It might be worth noting that Tintern Abbey is situated only a few miles from the Forest of Dean and is even seen as a location in Potter's *Cold Lazarus*.

43 In Potter's *Joe's Ark* (BBC, 1974) a young girl slowly dies of cancer. Her father Joe is a devout Christian but he cannot reconcile her innocent death with his religious beliefs, as he battles to understand what sin she could have committed to deserve such a dreadful fate. The play is full of Romantic allusions and seems to explicitly investigate the notion of original sin (see Creeber, 1998a: 88–96).

44 The nightclub 'Skinskapes' was even changed to 'Moonglow' for no apparent reason.

45 Talking about *Lipstick on Your Collar*, which also used songs from the 1950s, Potter told Graham Fuller that 'I don't like fifties music very much' (cited by Fuller, 1993: 103).

46 After the huge success of *The Singing Detective* the BBC allowed Potter to direct *Blackeyes*, a disappointment for both writer and corporation. This was followed by *Secret Friends* (1992) (again, it was directed by Potter and almost sunk without a trace). After these two disasters Potter would never direct his work again.

Bibliography

Barrow, Simon, 'Stand, Take, Walk: God's Restoration of Our Humanity', see <www.simonbarrow.net/article72> (2003, last accessed July 2006).

Barthes, Roland, 'The Death of the Author', in *Image, Music, Text* (London: Fontana, 1977).

BBC, *Drama Connections: The Singing Detective* [documentary on the serial], first broadcast on BBC1, 1 November 2005.

Bondebjerg, Ib, 'Intertextuality and Metafiction: Genre and Narration in the Television Fiction of Dennis Potter', in M. Skormand and K. C. Schroder (eds), *Media Cultures: Reappraising Transnational Media* (London and New York: Routledge, 1992).

Bowie, Malcolm, *Freud, Proust and Lacan: Theory as Fiction* (Cambridge and New York: Cambridge University Press, 1987).

Brooker, Peter, *A Glossary of Cultural Theory* (London: Arnold, 1999).

Canby, Vincent, 'Is This Year's Best Film on TV?', *The New York Times* (Arts and Leisure Section), 10 July, 1988.

Carpenter, Humphrey, *Dennis Potter: The Authorized Biography* (London: Faber & Faber, 1998).

Carroll, Robert and Prickett, Stephen, 'Introduction' to *The Bible: Authorized King James Version* (Oxford: Oxford University Press, 1997).

Caughie, John, *Television Drama: Realism, Modernism and British Culture* (Oxford and New York: Oxford University Press, 2000).

Cawelti, J., *Adventure, Mystery and Romance* (Chicago: University of Chicago Press, 1976).

Chandler, Raymond, *The Simple Act of Murder* (New York: Random House, orig. pub. 1934; 1988).

Cook, John, *Dennis Potter: A Life on Screen* (Manchester: Manchester University Press, 1998; first edn 1995).

Corrigan, Timothy, 'Music from Heaven, Bodies in Hell: *The Singing Detective*', in *A Cinema Without Walls: Movies and Culture after Vietnam* (London: Routledge, 1991).

Coveney, Peter, *Poor Monkey: The Child in Literature* (London: Rockcliff, 1957).

Creeber, Glen, 'Banality with a Beat: Dennis Potter and the Paradox of Popular Music', *Media, Culture and Society* vol. 18 no. 3, July 1996.

Creeber, Glen, *Dennis Potter: Between Two Worlds: A Critical Reappraisal* (London and New York: Macmillan, 1998a).

Creeber, Glen, ' "Reality of Nothing": Dennis Potter's *Cold Lazarus*', in Mike Wayne (ed.), *Dissident Voices: The Politics of Television and Social Change* (London: Pluto Press, 1998b).

Creeber, Glen, ' "The Anxious and the Uprooted": Dennis Potter and Richard Hoggart, Scholarship Boys', in Vernon W. Gras and John R. Cook (eds), *The Passion of Dennis Potter: International Collected Essay* (New York: St Martin's Press, 2000).

Creeber, Glen, *Serial Television: Big Drama on the Small Screen* (London: BFI, 2004).

De Abaitua, Matthew, 'Review of *The Singing Detective* [film version]', <Channel 4.com/film/reviews> (last accessed July 2006).

Delany, Paul, 'Potterland', *Dalhousie Review* vol. 68 part 4 (1988).

Eco, Umberto, *The Role of the Reader* (Indiana: Indiana Press, 1979).

Evans, Dave, 'Clenched Fists: The Official Dennis Potter Website', <www.yorksj.ac.uk/potter> (last accessed July 2006).

Fenichel, Otto, *The Psychoanalytical Theory of Neurosis* (London: Routledge & Kegan Paul, 1966).

Fisher, Mark, 'Gothic Oedipus: Subjectivity and Capitalism in Christopher Nolan's *Batman Begins*', *Image Text, Interdisciplinary Comic Studies* vol. 2 no. 2, Winter. See <web.english.ufl.edu/imagetext/archives/v2_2/ fisher/#9> (last accessed July 2006).

Fraim, John, 'Palace of Illusion: The Rise and Fall of a Grand Mythology', <www.expertson.com/Branding_Symbolism/palaceofillusion.html> (2002, last accessed July 2006).

Freud, Sigmund, *Civilization and Its Discontents*, Standard Edition, XXI (London: The Hogarth Press, 1930).

Freud, Sigmund, 'Contributions to the Psychology of Love: The Most Prevalent Form of Degradation in Erotic Life', in *Collected Papers Vol. IV* (London: The Hogarth Press, 1954).

Freud, Sigmund, *Introduction of Lectures on Psychoanalysis* (London: Penguin Books, 1976).

Freud, Sigmund, *On Sexuality* (London: Penguin, 1977).

Frye, Northrop, *Fearul Symmetry: A Study of William Blake* (Princeton: Princeton University Press, 1967).

Fuller, Graham (ed.), *Potter on Potter* (London: Faber & Faber, 1993).

Gilbert, W. Stephen, *Fight & Kick & Bite: The Life and Work of Dennis Potter* (London: Hodder & Stoughton, 1995).

Gould, Tony, *Don't Fence Me In: From Curse to Cure, Leprosy in Modern Times* (London: Bloomsbury Press, 2005).

Gras, Vernon, 'Dennis Potter's *The Singing Detective*: An Exemplum of Dialogical Ethics', in Vernon W. Gras and John R. Cook (eds), *The Passion of Dennis Potter: International Collected Essays* (New York: St Martin's Press, 2000).

Heavenor, E. S. P., 'Job', in D. Guthrie and J. A. Motyer (eds), *New Bible Commentary*, third edn (Leicester: Inter-Varsity, 1970).

Hilfer, Antony, ' "Run Over by One's Own Story": Genre and Ethos in Dennis Potter's *The Singing Detective*', in Jonathan Bignell, Stephen Lacey and Madeleine Macmurraugh-Kavanagh (eds), *British Television Drama: Past, Present and Future* (London: Palgrave, 2000).

Hunningher, Joost, '*The Singing Detective*: Who Done It?', in George W. Brandt (ed.), *British Television Drama in the 1980s* (Cambridge: Cambridge University Press, 1993).

Jacobs, Jason, 'Hospital Drama', in Glen Creeber (ed.), *The Television Genre Book* (London: BFI, 2001).

Jameson, Fredric, *The Prison-House of Language* (Princeton: Princeton University Press, 1972).

Kierkegaard, Soren, *The Journals of Soren Kierkegaard* (Princeton: Princeton University Press, 1983).

King, Steven, 'Television & Radio', *The Times*, 1 May 2004.

Lichtenstein, Therese, 'Syncopated Thriller: Dennis Potter's *The Singing Detective*', *Artforum,* May 1990.

Lippard, Chris, 'Confined Bodies, Wandering Minds: Memory, Paralysis and the Self in Some Earlier Works of Dennis Potter', in Vernon W. Gras and John R.

Cook (eds), *The Passion of Dennis Potter: International Collected Essays* (New York: St Martin's Press, 2000).

Malcolm, Derek, 'Home Defeat, Away Win', *The Guardian*, 22 April 1993.

Meter, Jan R. van, 'Sophocles and the Rest of the Boys in the Pulps: Myth and the Detective Novel', in Larry N. Landrum, Pat Browne and Ray B. Browne (eds), *Dimensions of Detective Fiction* (Bowling Green, O.H.: Popular Press, 1976).

Meyer, Nicholas, *The Seven-Per-Cent Solution* (London and New York: W. W. Norton & Company, 1974).

Milton, John, *Paradise Lost* (Cambridge: Cambridge University Press, orig. pub. 1674; 2001).

Mitchell, Juliet, *Psychoanalysis and Feminism* (London: Penguin, 1974).

Nelson, Robin, *Television in Transition: Forms, Values and Cultural Change* (London: Macmillan, 1987).

O'Connor, John J., 'Creator of Detective', *The New York Times*, 14 January 1988.

Pederson-Krag, Geraldine, 'Detective Stories and the Primal Scene', in Larry N. Landrum, Pat Browne and Ray B. Browne (eds), *Dimensions of Detective Fiction* (Bowling Green, O.H.: Popular Press, orig. pub. 1949; 1976).

Place, Janey, 'Women in Film Noir', in E. Ann Kaplan (ed.), *Women in Film Noir* (London: BFI, 1986).

Plater, Alan, 'Sex, Television Drama and the Writer', included in Andrea Millwood Hargrave (ed.), *British Broadcasting Standards Council, Annual Review, 1992: Sex and Sexuality in Broadcasting* (London: John Libbey Press, 1992).

Potter, Dennis, *The Glittering Coffin* (London: Gollancz, 1960).

Potter, Dennis, *Hide and Seek* (London: Faber & Faber, 1973).

Potter, Dennis, 'Realism and Non-Naturalism 2', *The Official Programme of the Edinburgh International Television Festival*, August 1977.

Potter, Dennis, *The Singing Detective* (London: Faber & Faber, 1986).

Potter, Dennis, 'Some Sort of Preface . . .', in *Waiting for the Boat: On Television* (London: Faber & Faber, 1987).

Potter, Dennis, *Seeing the Blossom: Two Interviews and a Lecture* (London: Faber & Faber, 1994).

Potter, Dennis, *Karaoke and Cold Lazarus* (London: Faber & Faber, 1996).

Prys, Catrin, 'The Singing Detective', in Glen Creeber (ed.), *50 Key Television Programmes* (London: Arnold, 2004).

Prys, Catrin, 'Issues in Television Authorship', in Glen Creeber (ed.), *Tele-Visions: An Introduction to Studying Television* (London: BFI, 2006a).

Prys, Catrin, 'The Television Plays of Dennis Potter: An Investigation into the Aesthetics & Polysemy of Television Drama', unpublished PhD, University of Wales, Aberystwyth, 2006b.

Prys, Catrin, 'Don't Fence Me In: *The Singing Detective* and the Synchronicity of Indeterminacy', in Laura Mulvey and Jamie Sexton, *Experimental Television* (Manchester: Manchester University Press, forthcoming).

Scott, A. O., 'A Pulp Novelist's Dreams Invade a Distressing Reality', *The New York Times*, Sunday, 14 May 2006.

Seiter, Ellen, 'Semiotics, Structuralism and Television', in Robert C. Allen (ed.), *Channels of Discourse: A Reassessment* (London and New York: Routledge, 1992).

Shakespeare, Nicolas, 'Series With Massive Promise', *The Times*, 1 December 1986a.

Shakespeare, Nicolas, 'Music to my Eyes', *The Times*, 22 December 1986b.

Silver, Alain and Ward, Elizabeth (eds), *Film Noir* (New York: Secker & Warburg, 1980).

Spencer, Meagan, 'Review of *The Singing Detective*', <www.abc.au/Triplej/review/film/s1154907> (accessed 2006).

Stead, Peter, *Dennis Potter* (Bridgend: Seren Books, 1993).

Trodd, Kenith, 'Whose Dennis is it Anyway?', in Vernon W. Gras and John R. Cook (eds), *The Passion of Dennis Potter: International Collected Essays* (New York: St Martin's Press, 2000).

Tulloch, John, *Television Drama: Agency, Audience and Myth* (London and New York: Routledge, 1990).

Voigts-Virchow, Eckart, ' "Cornucopia of Tinsel": Dennis Potter and the Culture of Advertising', in Vernon W. Gras and John R. Cook (eds), *The Passion of Dennis Potter: International Collected Essays* (New York: St Martin's Press, 2000).

Wallach, Rick, 'Socialist Allegory in Dennis Potter's *Lipstick on Your Collar*', in Vernon W. Gras and John R. Cook (eds), *The Passion of Dennis Potter: International Collected Essays* (New York: St Martin's Press, 2000).

Williams, Hugo, 'With Knobs On', *New Statesman*, 28 November 1986.

Wordsworth, William, *The Works of William Wordsworth* (Hertfordshire: The Wordsworth Press, 1974).

Wu, Duncan, 'Dennis Potter: The Angel in Us', in *Six Contemporary British Dramatists: Bennett, Potter, Gray, Brenton, Hare, Ayckbourn* (London: Macmillan, 1995).

Wyver, John, 'A World Where the Songs Come True', included in *The Television Plays of Dennis Potter*, the brochure that accompanied a complete retrospective of Potter's work at the Museum of Television & Radio, New York, 1992.

Zoonen, Liesbet van, *Feminist Media Studies* (London, Thousand Oaks and New Delhi: Sage, 1994).

Zupancic, Alenka, *Ethics of the Real: Kant, Lacan* (London and New York: Verso, 2000).

Credits

The Singing Detective

A BBC (British Broadcasting Corporation) Television Production in association with ABC (Australian Broadcasting Corporation). First broadcast in the UK on BBC1, 16 November–21 December, 1986; Episode 1: 'Skin'; Episode 2: 'Heat'; Episode 3: 'Lovely Days'; Episode 4: 'Clues'; Episode 5: 'Pitter Patter'; Episode 6: 'Who Done It'. Approximately 70 minutes each episode.

writer
Dennis Potter
director
Jon Amiel
producers
Kenith Trodd
John Harris
Rick McCallum
designer
Jim Clay
photography
Ken Westbury
film editors
Sue Wyatt (episodes 1, 3, 5)
Bill Wright (episodes 4, 6)
music adviser
Max Harris
film editing
Bill Wright
Sue Wyatt
choreographer
Quinny Sacks
casting
Michelle Guish
visual effects designer
Mat Irvine
costume design
John Peacock
Hazel Pethig
make-up artists
Lesley Hamon
Fae Hammond

make-up designer
Frances Hannon
graphic/title designer
Joanna Ball
graphics
Mark Thomas
camera operator
Nigel Slatter
steadicam operator
John Ward
production associate
Ian Brindle
production assistant
Diana Brookes
production managers
Rosemary Padvaiskas
Michael Darbon
sound recordist
Clive Derbyshire
dubbing mixers
Rob James
Sue Metcalfe
sound editor
Colin Ritchie
boom operator
John Taylor
properties buyer
David Morris
gaffer
Sid Morris
script supervisor
Diana Brookes
colourist
Alan Bishop
clapper loader
James Moss
assistant floor managers
Lynda Pannett
Garry Boon
Nick Wise
Anna Price

cast
Michael Gambon
Philip E. Marlow
Janet Suzman
Nicola
Patrick Malahide
Mark Binney/Finney/Raymond

Joanne Whalley
Nurse Mills
Bill Paterson
Dr Gibbon
Jim Carter
Mr Marlow
Alison Steadman
Mrs Marlow/Lili
Lyndon Davies
young Philip
David Ryall
Mr Hall
Gerard Horan
Reginald
Imelda Staunton
Staff Nurse White
Mary McLeod
Sister Malone
Ron Cook
first mysterious man
George Rossi
second mysterious man
Geff Francis
hospital porter
Badi Uzzaman
Ali
Sharon D. Clarke
night nurse
Kate McKenzie
Sonia/prostitute
Charon Bourke
Amanda
Simon Chandler
Dr Finlay
Leslie French
Mr Tomkey, 'Noddy'
Charles Simon
George Adams
Janet Henfrey
schoolteacher/scarecrow
Nigel Pegram
busker
Richard Pescud
consultant
Thomas Wheatley
registrar
Paul Lacoux
houseman
John Matshikiza

visiting doctor
Joan White
Mrs Adams
Richard Butler
Grancher
Maggie Holland
Gran
Errol Shaker
first mortuary attendant
Astley Harvey
second mortuary attendant
Claire Phelps
Rita
Neil Pittaway
Brian
Niven Boyd
first soldier
David Thewlis
second soldier
Ken Stott
Uncle John
Angela Curran
Mary
Heather Tobia
girl evangelist/Nurse Godfrey
John Sheraton
drummer
Emma Myant
first hostess
Susie Ann Watkins
second hostess
Tricia George
physiotherapist
Samantha Bryant
Barbara
William Speakman
Mark Binney, aged 10

songs
'Peg o' my Heart' (series title music) by Fisher, performed by Max Harris and his Novelty Trio; 'Limehouse Blues' by Furber, Braham, performed by Ambrose and his Orchestra; 'Deutschland über Alles' by Hoffman, Fullersleben, soloist

Tommy Riley; 'House of Mystery'; 'I've Got You Under My Skin' by Porter, performed by Henry Hall Orchestra; 'Blues in the Night' by Arlen, Mercer, performed by Anne Shelton; 'Sunnyside of the Street' by Fields, McHugh; 'Entry of the Queen of Sheba' by G. F. Handel, performed by Christopher Hogwood; 'Dry Bones' by Livingstone Gearhart, performed by Fred Waring and the Pennsylvanians; 'Night and Day' by Porter; 'Rocking in Rhythm' by Ellington, Carney, Mills, peformed by Duke Ellington and his Famous Orchestra; 'Cruising Down the River' by Beadell, Tolleaton, performed by Michael Gambon, also by Lou Preager and his Orchestra, with Pul Rich; 'Don't Fence Me In' by Porter, performed by Bing Crosby and the Andrew Sisters; 'It Might as Well be Spring' by Rodgers, Hammerstein, performed by Dick Haymes; 'Rustle of Spring' by Sinding, performed by Joseph Cooper; 'Rocking on Rhythm'; 'Birdsong at Eventide' by Coates, performed by Ronnie Rondale; 'Paper Doll' by Black, performed by Mills Brothers; 'Lili Marlene' by Schultze, Leip, Conner, performed by Lale Anderson; 'Do I Worry' by Cowan, Worth, performed by the Ink Spots; 'Lili Marlene' peformed by Lale Anderson; 'Bei mir bist du Schön' by Secunda, Cahn, Chaplin, Jacobs, performed

by Maurice Winnick and his Sweet Music; 'Rockin' in Rhythm'; 'It's a Lovely Day Tomorrow' by Berlin, performed by Jack Payne and his Orchestra; 'I Get Along Without You Very Well' by Carmichael, performed by Sam Browne with Lew Stone Band; 'Life at its Best is Very Brief' by Kirkpatrick, organist Dennis Plowright; 'Ac-cent-tchu-ate the Positive' by Arlen, Mercer, performed by Bing Crosby and the Andrew Sisters; 'The Umbrella Man' by Rose, Stock, Cavanagh, performed by Sammy Kaye and his Orchestra with the Three Barons; 'Henrietta' by Featherstonehaugh, performed by Buddy Featherstonehaugh; 'You Always Hurst the One You Love' by Roberts, Fisher, performed by Mills Brothers; 'Ah! Sweet Mystery of Life' by Herbert, Young, performed by Ambrose and his Orchestra; 'After You've Gone' by Creamer, Layton, performed by Al Jolson; 'Into Each Life Some Rain Must Fall' by Roberts, Fisher, performed by Ella Fitzgerald and the Ink Spots; 'Putting on the Ritz' by Berlin, performed by Eric Rogers; 'The Very Thought of You' by Noble, performed by Al Bowlly with Ray Noble Orchestra; 'Teddy Bears' Picnic' by Tommy Reilly; 'We'll Meet Again' by Parker, Charles, performed by Vera Lynn with Arthur Young at the Novachord

Index

Page numbers in *italic* refer to illustrations; *n* = endnote

153